LAST CALL FOR
HMS *EDINBURGH*

Frank Pearce was born in Plymouth and educated at the
Hoe Grammar School. In the 1930s he was appointed as
the Devon County Amateur Swimming Association's
professional coach. Joining the navy soon after war broke
out he served as a gunner aboard merchant ships on
Atlantic convoy routes before joining the new cruiser
Trinidad commissioning in Devonport in 1941. He
served in her until she was lost while escorting a Russian
convoy in May 1942.

After the war he became a schoolmaster and latterly
a hotelier before devoting his retirement to painting and
writing.

Best wishes

FRANK PEARCE

LAST CALL FOR HMS *EDINBURGH*

A story of the Russian convoys

Pan Books
in association with
Collins

First published 1982 by William Collins Sons & Co. Ltd
This edition published 1982 by Pan Books Ltd,
Cavaye Place, London SW10 9PG
in association with William Collins Sons & Co. Ltd
© Frank Pearce 1982
ISBN 0 330 26686 1
Printed and bound in Great Britain by
Hazell Watson & Viney Ltd, Aylesbury, Bucks

This book is dedicated
to the men of
HMS *Edinburgh*

Acknowledgements

The author acknowledges with gratitude the contributions provided by many *Edinburgh* survivors and those closely associated with the events, among whom are:

Vice-Admiral Sir Arthur Fitzroy-Talbot, KBE, CB, DSO and Bar, DL, RN (Retd)

Vice-Admiral Sir George Raper, KCB, CB, RN (Retd)

Commander P. H. T. Rees, RN (Retd)

Commander J. Johnson, RN (Retd)

Commander A. J. Bailey, OBE, RN (Retd)

Lieut-Commander C. R. H. Broadway, RN

Paymaster Lieut-Commander B. C. M. McLean (Retd)

Lieut-Commander K. V. Burnes, RN (Retd)

Alan Devoud	Charles Long
Edwin Dennerley	Frank Woodley
Arthur Start	Williams Smitham
William Wallis	Frank Hodges
Leonard Bradley	Reginald Levick
Maurice Pascoe	Percy Jefford
William Fiddick	James Doyle
Harry Cook	William Daly
Reginald Phillips	James Harper
Wynn Jones	George Stripe
Ronald Bennett	

It is also a great pleasure to acknowledge the help given by the following.

Richard Ollard of Collins Publishers, who gave generously of his time and energy to promote the book.

My son Derek for story contribution.

Baron Jay Limited of Plymouth, publishers of the book *The Ship that Torpedoed Herself*, for their co-operation.

Dr P. D. Slater of Falmouth, the staffs of Plymouth and Falmouth Libraries and Alan Morris and Nigel Trevenna of Century Litho, Falmouth.

Contents

Illustrations

Icing on the upper deck
(Imperial War Museum)

HMS *Edinburgh* with *Sheffield* and *Kenya*
(Imperial War Museum)

A convoy to Russia under attack
(Imperial War Museum)

Part of the dockyard at Rosta in the Kola inlet

Walrus aircraft
(Imperial War Museum)

Captain Faulkner and Rear-Admiral Bonham-Carter

The German destroyer *Hermann Schoemann* on fire and sinking

HMS *Edinburgh* looking aft

Foreword

THIS IS THE TRUE STORY of the *Edinburgh* – a proud and brave ship that refused to accept defeat and died in a blaze of glory. Crippled, sinking, defiant to the last, her guns blazed destruction on an enemy which although superior in armament withdrew in fear and dismay.

But, within this story there were other ships, tiny ships, in this sea drama of World War II which, although outgunned and outnumbered, fought with a gallantry worthy of the finest traditions of the Royal Navy.

Now, nearly forty years from 2 May 1942, when she slid with dignity beneath the waters of the Arctic Ocean flaunting her battle ensign, the cruiser *Edinburgh* is remembered again but for a totally different reason. For from within the bowels of her rusting, rotting hull and the tomb of those who died with her the major part of a vast fortune in gold bullion estimated to be worth £45 million has now been recovered. Yet until recently, few people knew that *Edinburgh* was transporting gold from Russia to the United Kingdom at the time she was sunk.

Fresh salvage attempts may be made to recover the remainder of the bullion from the floorbed of the Barents Sea within the Arctic circle. But it is not as a treasure ship that *Edinburgh* is to be remembered, not for her gold but rather her gallantry, not her fortune but her fortitude.

Perhaps this book will help establish the story of *Edinburgh* and her escorts in its rightful place in British naval history.

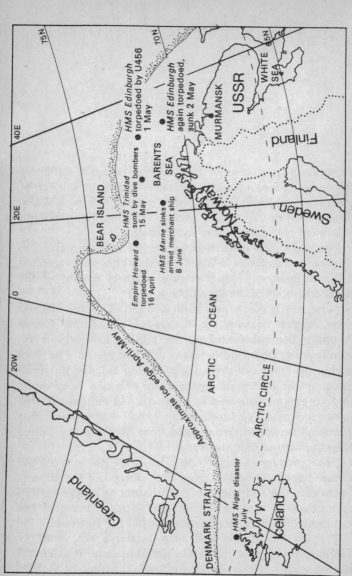

General map showing areas of action between 16 April and 4 July 1942.

Introduction

AT THE BEGINNING of World War II, as the German armies drove deeper and deeper into the heart of Russia, destroying factories and armament industries, that country's capabilities of redeeming her losses for its defence became critical. The British Prime Minister, Winston Churchill and the President of the United States of America, Franklin D. Roosevelt had promised the Soviet leader Joseph Stalin that, primarily under a lend–lease agreement, the Allies would supply guns, tanks, planes and other equipment as far as resources would allow. The shortest route to provide these war materials to the hard-pressed Russians was through the Arctic Ocean from Iceland to Murmansk. There were two other routes, both overland but both painfully slow. This was the most direct and the most dangerous.

Thus was created the 2000 mile convoy route through the Arctic Ocean which soon became known as 'The Gateway to Hell'. In a determined attempt to stop these supplies getting through, the German Chancellor Adolf Hitler had established an impressive number of submarine, destroyer and airforce bases along the northern coast of Norway.

Between Iceland and North Russia lies one of the most tempestuous areas of water in the world. Over this ocean endless gales, bringing sleet, snow and hail whip up the sea into a succession of frightening waves which hurl themselves in fury upon any ship in their path. Optional convoy alterations in course to try to avoid enemy action were greatly reduced by drift ice forming the northern boundary of this storm-bound sea and moving so far south at times that its edge would leave a navigable stretch of water only 80 miles wide between it and North Cape. From their bases here the enemy could operate without difficulty, attacking each convoy battling its way eastward or westward.

At times, navigation became almost impossible as freezing spray from great waves fell upon each ship forming a layer of ice so thick that small ships could become unstable and capsize. In winter, when darkness persisted almost continuously throughout the twenty-four hours, ships had to navigate without lights and still maintain convoy formation. It became a nightmarish experience. But when summer days came and the midnight sun never set, the enemy was able to attack unceasingly throughout the twenty-four hours of daylight leaving gun crews and bridge personnel exhausted. The story of the Russian convoys became a living legend, the battle of the Arctic Ocean a war apart, a sea conflict at the top of the world which only those who were actively involved could really understand.

For the men who manned the ships it was a personal war. Personal, because firstly it brought a comradeship imposed by conditions, and later as each man became an essential part of a highly efficient fighting unit, they found they were utterly dependent upon one another. Few were spurred by patriotism; most saw it as one way to protect their families and all they held dear against the terror of Hitler domination, a way of preserving the little cottage in Devon or the terrace house in Manchester, which was to them, home. The largest proportion were civilians, conscripted from every walk of life. Financiers and farmers, plumbers and poets, coalmen and chemists, solicitors and steeplejacks. They were all there. A few weeks' training and suddenly with almost merciless haste they were at sea learning the hard way; mere amateurs conditioned by bitter experience to become professionals. In action there were few disputes and no shirkers. Every man did his job with all the strength and ability he could muster. He had to, for each fought for his own survival and the survival of the ship – an elongated floating box of steel plating – all that kept them from the freezing sea on which they floated and into which, if a man were suddenly plunged would kill in minutes.

But there were other factors eroding the will to endure. Not least, fear. The fear of being trapped below decks in a sinking ship. An anxiety that develops and expands with the knowledge that only thin steel plating lies between you and the cold black water rushing past. The terror that sets the heart pounding as every instinct warns that a torpedo might come smashing through the inadequate protection to bring choking death in impenetrable blackness.

And there was exhaustion. Physical and mental, brought about by lack of sleep. Hour after hour closed up at action stations, numbed with cold and plagued by sea-sickness, the constant demand took its toll. There were days of crushing tension when men could only be fed with cocoa and sandwiches at their positions. Nights of never ending alarms brought about by continual 'asdic' contacts – a technical device providing a warship with the capability of detecting enemy submarines lurking under the sea but bringing a fatigue which screamed for a man to let go, if only for a minute or two, to close his eyelids for a few precious seconds. Yet from deep within, a nagging voice that told him he could not, dare not, knowing that in one moment of inattention he could endanger the ship, his mates and probably subscribe to his own destruction. Added to this, was the constant rolling as the vessel lurched and pitched in heavy seas. Wrapped in duffel coats, jerseys, scarves, balaclava helmets and padded with layers of underclothes, pom-pom gun crews, signalmen and look-outs still shivered as they tried to screen themselves from the bitter Arctic wind and sleet. Hour after hour men wrapped their arms round rails and braced their feet against anything bolted down to prevent being flung across a steel deck or against a sharp cornered stanchion. The penalty of forgetfulness or carelessness was a cut lip or a split ear or most likely a twisted ankle. Sometimes it was all these things together.

Escort and merchant ships shuddered under the impact of enormous waves that reared up into awesome mountains of water. Deep in the troughs the quiet seemed uncanny. Then followed the long haul climbing slowly, crab-like to the peak of another foam-lashed crest, there to re-encounter the unharnessed force of the tempest, tearing and screaming like a thousand devils. Binoculars became useless as rain and sleet froze on the lenses. Guns and torpedoes, rendered unusable under the weight of frozen spray, required constant attention to keep them operational.

In exposed conditions on the upper deck, wind-whipped snow and sleet formed icicles on the faces of officers and men on watch. It was a time when human endurance was called for from every man, no matter what his station. Even when a brief spell of sleep could be permitted for part of the watch, men declined to sling their hammocks, preferring to sleep fully clothed and gloved, propped up against hammock racks or near steam pipes to gain a little warmth. No man in his right mind ever undressed on the Arctic convoy run. The bulky garments he wore would keep him afloat for a few minutes at least. If he wasn't rescued in that time he would be dead anyway.

It is against this background that the story of *Edinburgh* takes place, in an ocean where convoys of defenceless merchant ships escorted by the Royal Navy sailed back and forth almost on the enemy's doorstep, in defiance of whatever attacks the Nazis could mount.

CHAPTER 1

Arctic Convoy PQ14 Eastward

THE OCCUPATION OF ICELAND by American forces in July 1941 proved to be one of the most successful strategic moves made by the Allies throughout the war. It established a base from which convoys could operate in their bid to aid the hard-pressed Russian armies. By early March 1942, twelve convoys, carrying badly needed war materials for the Soviet troops, had successfully battled their way through to North Russia with the loss of only one ship – the Royal Naval destroyer *Matabele*. This event was one of the most tragic of the Arctic war.

On 10 January 1942, convoy PQ8, consisting of eight ships loaded with tanks and guns for the Russian front had set out from Iceland for the North Russian port of Murmansk. The protecting escort comprised the new cruiser *Trinidad* commanded by Captain Leslie S. Saunders, two destroyers *Matabele* and *Somali*, and two minesweepers *Speedwell* and *Harrier*. At this time of year, the long hours of darkness and the incessant gales somewhat reduced the threat of successful enemy action. Slowly the convoy proceeded on its voyage through the dark Arctic waters, while the escorts circled the perimeter of the little fleet of merchantmen, each vessel fighting its own battle with the constant storms, ploughing into great seas, climbing to foaming crests or dropping crazily into the troughs with 30 to 40 degrees reading on the roll indicators. Of all seasons of the year, this was the worst for man's survival against the seas and freezing spray. Steam heating within ships comfortably increased the temperature but because of icy conditions outside, with the temperature at 35 degrees below freezing and with deadlights screwed down over the portholes, condensation in the messdecks became excessive. The atmosphere soon became fetid and parts of the inside of the hull grew a thick green mildew. In such conditions, sleeping close together, the slightest infectious ailment could become an epidemic. It is true to say that the Arctic in wartime produced a background of fear, fear of what might happen if the ship should be torpedoed and one had to take to the rafts, or worse, how quickly death would come if it meant trying to swim for it. Here in this harsh desolate sea, framed by great ice masses and unpopulated lands, the most buoyant spirit became depressed. The pitiless cold, the savage sea, the pervading loneliness and the brutal enemy all banded together to undermine the will to endure.

By Sunday 17 January, the convoy and its escorts were approaching the North Russian coast, close to the Kola inlet, in darkness. These were the most dangerous waters where enemy submarines gathered in force to intercept the incoming merchant ships. At 7.45 that evening, asdic contacts showed submarines to be converging on the convoy. Just before 8 o'clock there was a violent explosion which lit up the night sky. The leading merchant ship *Harmatris* had been torpedoed. The explosion occurred near the bow of the ship where part of the cargo consisted of torpedo warheads, each containing approximately 300 lbs of high explosive. By a miracle, the warheads fell through the bottom of the ship without detonating. In the same hold was a large quantity of warm clothing intended for distribution to Polish internees which, blown upwards through the deck, became entangled in the rigging – as if the ship were dressed overall with jerseys, pants, scarves and every conceivable sort of garment instead of the usual bunting of flags.

In the meantime, the destroyers *Matabele* and *Somali* dashed around the convoy at high speed dropping depth charges to deter the U boats from attacking. But ignoring the British destroyers, the U boat commander moved ahead of the convoy hoping to repeat his earlier success and three hours later, having positioned himself in the path of the oncoming convoy, he fired two torpedoes which found their target in the magazines of *Matabele*. Here, far below the water-line, deep under the gun turrets, the magazine steel-lined chambers contained a store of explosive cordite and shells. An immense sheet of flame, some 700 feet high, shot into the air in an incandescent glare followed by a curtain of red hot debris slowly falling back into the sea. In seconds, nothing of the ship remained except for floating fragments of furniture and clothing. Scores of her crew of two hundred had been hurled into the water but this was followed by another catastrophe. Several of the destroyer's own depth charges, primed to explode at certain depths ready for their next attack, now blew up beneath those in the sea who were still alive.

The minesweeper *Harrier* raced in to try to pick up survivors. Her task was difficult and harrowing, for the icy wind bringing the temperature to 30 degrees below freezing produced a thin swirling fog which froze like hoar frost. The decks were by now a mass of ice and lowering the rescue boat with the ropes and pulleys frozen solid was a tough and exhausting task. When eventually the boat was lowered the crew rowed towards the disaster area in the darkness. Here they found the sea covered with a thick layer of oil fuel spilled out from the destroyer's tanks. Steering through the debris, they were just able to distinguish numbers of men in their life jackets, floating upright but quite dead. As the crew rowed on they found the surface littered with men in this gruesome state, victims of the explosions and the freezing water. Approaching, they found the oil so thick they could hardly move the boat. The oars were dipping into a mass of thick sludge and getting them nowhere.

Not far away they heard men calling for help but it was impossible to go further. From somewhere behind them they heard a chorus of faint shouts. Spurred on by the cries they went astern and within minutes found three men together and still alive. They were enveloped in thick oil and the task of hauling them aboard was formidable for they were much too weak to help themselves and in their slippery condition it was difficult to find a handhold.

Eventually the crew pulled back to *Harrier* and there the survivors were embarked, which was only accomplished after scrambling nets had been lowered and heaving lines passed around the chests of the three men who by now were almost unconscious. By the time they had been carried into the wardroom for medical attention all three had passed out. An hour later one was found to be dead but the other two recovered. Thus, out of the total crew of two hundred only two men survived.

Convoys to North Russia at this time were numbered bearing the prefix letters PQ and those returning QP. In the early period there was an acute shortage of anti-submarine escorts and all the protection a convoy could expect from the Royal Navy was one cruiser, two destroyers, one minesweeper and two trawlers, the latter to pick up survivors. By April 1942 the situation had changed substantially. The numbers of escorts had increased but against this so had the size of the convoys.

On 6 April 1942, there assembled at Reykjavik in the south-west corner of Iceland the biggest convoy yet marshalled to attempt the hazardous voyage to Murmansk. This was PQ14 and bore the codeword 'Credence'. Its cruiser escort was to be *Edinburgh*, then anchored at Scapa Flow and waiting to join. The 10,000 ton cruiser was one of two of this type – *Belfast* being the other. Attached to the

Home Fleet *Edinburgh* presented a formidable deterrent to the enemy. Six hundred and thirteen feet long with a sixty-three foot beam and an extensive fo'c'sle deck running beyond the bridge, she fully justified the impression of being a capable and dangerous fighting ship. Built at Wallsend in 1938 she was commissioned with the Home Fleet in 1939 close to the outbreak of war and commanded by one of the most popular captains in the Royal Navy, Captain Hugh Faulkner, later to become Rear-Admiral Faulkner, CB, CBE, DSO.* Into this ship had been incorporated all that was best of modern technical equipment, which with the men, weapons and machinery had been integrated into a highly sophisticated fighting unit. Apart from the most up-to-date asdic equipment to detect submarines, she carried the latest in radar detection. Ceaselessly the masthead scanners swept the horizon so that nothing was secure from its sensitive probe. Aircraft, ships, even a surfaced U boat, all could be detected within its range. And once the enemy was located speed became the essential factor. *Edinburgh* was well equipped in this field. Powered by Parson's geared turbines developing 80,000 horse power, she was officially estimated to have a speed of 33 knots but unofficially could reach 37 knots.

In her role as a fighting ship, both in attack and defence her destructive capability was highly significant. If the

*During his years in the Royal Navy, Captain Faulkner had a distinguished career rising rapidly in the promotion list. Born in 1900, he served as a midshipman aboard the HMAS *Australia* in 1916 in the First World War. He secured his captaincy in 1940 when he took over as commanding officer of HMS *Edinburgh*. During the North African and Sicily landings in 1942–43, he was mentioned in despatches four times, was appointed Director of Naval Combined Operations from 1943 to 1945, and Chief of Staff to the Allied Naval Expeditionary Forces with the rank of commodore in 1945. He was then given command of the aircraft carrier HMS *Triumph* and from 1948–49 was Captain of the Royal Naval College at Dartmouth. In 1949 he was promoted to Rear-Admiral and became Flag Officer of the Malayan Area in 1950. His retirement due to ill-health followed in 1952.

enemy appeared he would be pursued, attacked and destroyed. That was *Edinburgh's* function. She had four triple turrets of 6-inch guns controlled from the director towers. These supplied the vital information required to give bearing, range etc, to the highly technical electronic computer tables in the transmitting station. Having received this data, the TS could then calculate, among many other things, enemy course and speed which then had to be converted into supplying the training and elevation angles to lay the guns on target. Even the temperature of the air could affect the flight of shells and these ballistic details had to be allowed for. Once the computer had evaluated the information, directions were relayed to the guns, constantly bringing them up to date in step with the changing situation. The location of this vital link in the armament control was sited to give the maximum protection to both the computer and its crew. It was placed deep in the bowels of the ship below an armoured plated deck surrounded in some ships by oil tanks. This covered the main armament. Additionally, she had twelve 4-inch guns, four three-pounders and sixteen smaller guns which could produce a most effective barrage of fire against any aircraft foolish enough to come within range. The 21-inch torpedoes, burnished and sinister and each charged with 750 lbs of TNT in its warhead, lay in the triple tubes housed on either side of the ship ready to be launched on their destructive errands. Behind the bridge superstructure, two vast hangars housed the Walrus aircraft. Immediately aft of the hangars, the launching catapult deck lying athwartships was identified by the incongruous lines of the port and starboard cranes to recover the aircraft from the sea.

This was the cruiser *Edinburgh*. A powerful, efficient and highly trained fighting unit of the Royal Navy, capable of inflicting grievous damage or destruction to an enemy ship.

Before leaving Scapa Flow, *Edinburgh* had been ordered to take aboard a most unusual cargo, a number of large steel

plates urgently needed to repair the disabled cruiser
Trinidad, now lying in dry dock in the Kola inlet near
Murmansk.

The torpedoing of *Trinidad* was in itself one of the most
extraordinary events of the war. *Trinidad* escording PQ13 to
Murmansk had encountered in fog three of Germany's most
powerful destroyers. A savage gun battle followed at point
blank range in which one of the enemy was destroyed and
another badly damaged. In this engagement *Trinidad* had
fired a torpedo which after speeding on its way to finish off
the enemy ship then circled back and exploded in her own
port side, killing 32 men and causing an alarming list. By dint
of skilled seamanship the cruiser managed to limp into the
Kola inlet and later docked at Rosta in the bay of Vaenga.
The Russians were quite prepared to supply the labour but
were unable to provide the plates necessary to patch the
great hole 60 ft by 20 ft in the cruiser's side. The plates were
apparently somewhere in the Rosta dockyard buried under
tons of snow.

The convoy now at Reykjavik comprised twenty-three
merchantmen carrying guns, tanks, planes, ammunition and
trucks. Of these ten were British, nine American, three
Russian and one Greek. The ships sailed at 1400 on
Wednesday 8 April 1942, accompanied by eight small
escorts of anti-submarine trawlers and armed minesweepers,
and made their way along the northern coast intending to
rendezvous with *Edinburgh* and a substantial destroyer and
corvette escort at a point north-east of the island, in position
69 degrees 10 north and 11 degrees 02 west at 1000, on
Sunday 12 April.

From this point, things began to go wrong. The convoy's
route had been chosen on the assumption that the Polar ice-
barrier would have receded to allow easy passage north-east
of the island. In fact it was further south than usual and on
Sunday morning the convoy and its escorts ran into thick
drifting ice. In the meantime *Edinburgh* flying the flag of

Rear-Admiral Sir Stuart Bonham-Carter KCB, CB, CVO, DSO, commanding the 18th cruiser squadron,* had left Scapa Flow. Making for the rendezvous point with her own escorts she encountered thick fog, which by midnight had shut down visibility altogether, and descended on the ships in a mass of swirling mist. Soon the fog was all around them, until from the bridge they could barely see the bows, much less the sea. It was only radar that kept the vessels from colliding with one another. On the glowing screen it showed precisely where each ship lay, so that without alteration in speed or course they moved steadily on to the appointed rendezvous.

But from the convoy escorts to the north, the admiral began to receive signals which were most disturbing. Three of the minesweeper force had sustained severe damage in collision with ice resulting in badly leaking compartments. Three anti-submarine trawlers reported their asdic-domes out of action and three more in critical condition were forced to return to Iceland to save the vessels from total loss. In the meantime the merchant ships, themselves in dense fog, had also entered the field of ice. Conditions became so bad that a confused and tense situation developed. The heavily loaded vessels found themselves surrounded by and colliding with, large solid tables of ice that threatened to engulf them. In some cases the ships were cannoning into a compact wall of the ice-field itself. It would have been bad enough in good visibility but in

---

* Born in 1889, the Admiral served throughout the First World War with great distinction. His exploits during this period earned him the awards of the French Legion of Honour and the Croix de Guerre, the Italian Silver Cross for Valour, the Belgian Croix de Guerre and the British DSO. During the years 1932 to 1934 he became Assistant Director of Naval Equipment and from 1937 to 1939 took command as Commodore of the Royal Naval Barracks, Chatham. At the beginning of the Second World War he was appointed Naval Secretary to the First Lord of the Admiralty, and later Rear-Admiral commanding the 18th Cruiser Squadron. Promoted to Vice-Admiral in 1943, he retired in 1944.

blanket fog it became a nightmare. Once in, they had to get out – but which way was out? Hulls became buckled, plates ruptured causing flooding, stems were crushed and pro-peller blades dismembered. It was a bad beginning to a voyage which had promised so much.

When the weather cleared and *Edinburgh* had joined the convoy it was seen, that only eight merchant ships were present with an impressive escort of six destroyers, four corvettes, four minesweepers and two trawlers. By Tuesday the 14th, with a third of the voyage completed there was the possibility that with luck they might escape detection but Admiral Bonham-Carter was under no illusion about the dangers that lay ahead. The following morning two of the accompanying destroyers *Foresight* and *Forester* picked up U boat contacts to north and south of the convoy. Racing to the areas, they dropped patterns of depth charges but without any apparent success. That evening a German reconnaissance plane found the convoy and shadowed it keeping well out of range. Almost immediately it proceeded to transmit homing signals to its Norwegian base giving the exact position and course of the merchant ships. From now on PQ14 knew that it must expect enemy attacks within hours.

By Thursday, the convoy was ten miles south of Bear Island, a remote spot near the 75 degree latitude and south of Spitzbergen. Now close against the ice barrier, any further movement to the north would find them locked in the ice-field from which there might be no escape. It was here that the Germans, anticipating the course, concentrated their U boats. Heavy black snow clouds drifting at sea level decreased visibility which was already poor. Almost at once escorts picked up on their radar screens enemy submarines, surfaced and waiting, obviously preparing to make a concerted attack. *Edinburgh* could do little to offset the danger or to assist the destroyers in their efforts to form a protective screen around the cargo ships. Her express function was to guard the convoy against surface attack, in particular from marauding enemy destroyers. It was clearly no place for a large cruiser markedly vulnerable to U boat attack and when tracks of torpedoes were seen crossing *Edinburgh*'s bows, the admiral ordered the ship to speed to the west. After signalling his intention to the senior officer of the close escorts, Commander Maxwell Richmond, OBE, commanding the destroyer *Bulldog,* HMS *Edinburgh* took up a position ten miles astern of the convoy. The convoy itself was now approaching one of the most dangerous zones of the voyage, and Commander Richmond, assuming full responsibility, then ordered the convoy ships to make a bold alteration of course to the southward.

This move allowed them to keep clear of the ice-field, dodge the closing U boats and avoid the probability of a minefield laid by the enemy in the predictable path of the convoy. It was a logical move and in the circumstances, the safest. Acknowledging, the commodore of the merchant ships, Captain Edward Rees, DSC, RD, RNR, aboard the cargo vessel *Empire Howard* carrying 2000 tons of military stores, put the order into operation. With a gross tonnage of 7000 tons she had been built at Port Glasgow and registered at Lloyds in 1941. This modern steamship 446 ft long and 56 ft wide with a single propeller had the traditional bridge amidships, two masts and a single funnel. A line of signals fluttered out from the mast followed by the 'execute' flag. Slowly at first, the vessels slewed around into line heading south, propellers thrashing the sea into white trails, labouring under the weight of their heavy cargoes.

At varying distances from and around the convoy, escorts were fully occupied chasing clear and strong U boat contacts. With funnels pouring black smoke and bow waves creaming back as they sliced through the dark grey sea, destroyers and corvettes circled and weaved above their targets. Pattern after pattern of depth charges erupted from the ocean to discharge awesome towers of foaming water.

The destroyers *Bulldog, Forester* and *Amazon* had several sightings of submarines on the surface but although *Forester*, the leading ship opened fire, the U boats crash-dived and contact was soon lost.

In this action Commander Richmond played a particularly prominent part in attacking the submerged U boats, weaving and turning his ship in tight circles to depth charge the enemy. Though no kills were established it succeeded in keeping the enemy's head down and away from the convoy.

Meanwhile, at the pre-determined speed of only 8 knots to conserve fuel, and with visibility at one and a half miles, the convoy plodded along in a formation of four columns of two ships each, with *Empire Howard* in the forward column. It will never be established whether the U boats deliberately revealed their presence on the surface in order to lure the escorts away but it is recorded that when the commodore saw the destroyers speeding off in pursuit he turned to the captain of the vessel, Captain Harold Downie, with the remark, 'I hope the escorts are not being decoyed away from us'. At that point, the merchant ships had as close escorts the two anti-submarine trawlers, *Lord Middleton* and *Northern Wave*, stationed three-quarters of a mile astern with the destroyer *Beverley* one mile ahead. But undetected, one U boat daringly closed in to penetrate the screen astern of *Beverley* and after selecting its target fired three torpedoes. The victim was the *Empire Howard*. No one saw the tracks of the deadly tin fish as they sped on their way, although just before the first torpedo struck Captain Downie described a noise like that of a plane, which must have been the torpedoes travelling through the water. There was a blinding flash as the first plunged into the starboard side, exploding in the boiler room. Five seconds later the second smashed its way through the engine room; ten seconds later the third struck between No 4 and 5 holds and the magazine exploded in a mighty eruption of flame, smoke and steam.

No vessel made could have withstood such an impact. The explosions tore out the centre of the vessel in a great flash, splitting her in two. The upper decks disappeared and with them the entire cargo of army trucks which fell into the sea with a grinding cacophony of noise and brought men to the rails of accompanying ships to stare in horror and disbelief. Immediately, *Empire Howard* started to sink stern first in a sea of white foaming water, her shattered hull screaming in protest. Within thirty seconds the water was up to the bridge ladders. In the few moments left, Captain Downie with the aid of the second mate and the naval radio telegraphist collected the confidential books stored in lead-weighted bags and threw them overboard. Then, shouting to the others to leave the ship he calmly stepped into a sea well below freezing point, wearing a life jacket. He had managed to scramble away some twenty yards when the bow of the ship reared up and slid under, stern first. It had been just sixty seconds from the time the first torpedo struck. Looking around through a pall of drifting black smoke all he could see was a vast circle of swirling water, its centre eddying and bubbling as air from the sunken ship burst to the surface bringing with it a mass of flotsam. As the smoke cleared, he saw that some of the crew who had survived the explosion were clinging to pieces of wreckage and to three small rafts which had floated off as the ship sank. In the lifting swell a survivor swept past him. It was the commodore, Captain Rees, a smile on his face, nonchalantly trying to smoke a cigar. Before they could reach one another a large roller bore him out of sight and he was never seen again. So died a brave man, who faced the inevitable with a fortitude and calmness given to few. Such was the sea temperature, one degree centigrade, that in normal circumstances the men in the water would have been dead in five minutes. They were however swimming around in a sea inches thick in oil fuel spilled out from the ship's tanks. It was undoubtedly this that kept them alive.

At the time of the explosion the two anti-submarine

trawlers astern of the convoy immediately altered course and raced towards the stricken vessel, their task twofold: to attack the U boat with depth charges and to rescue survivors. The *Northern Wave*, just outside the line of advance of the starboard column was the first to arrive, but thrashing about in the sea in the path of the trawler in an area of black oil and debris were thirty-eight men, waving, screaming and pleading to be saved. The young captain, Lieutenant William Pardoe-Matthews, RNR, was faced with an agonizing decision. The asdic-dome under the hull had been put out of action by ice damage at the beginning of the voyage. He had no means of confirming his belief that the U boat must be beneath them in the middle of the convoy. If he attacked it was certain that many of those in the water would be killed by the terrible concussion effect from the depth charges. If he did not, there could be another ship sunk, and another, and another. Logic argued that the U boat had to be there in the depths below for not enough time had elapsed to allow its escape. Should he ignore the presence of the submarine in order to save the survivors and thereby allow the enemy to slip away to kill and maim ten times that number? He was faced with an impossible choice which must have ravaged brain and heart like a searing flame. In taking command of *Northern Wave* the orders had been clear and specific, 'Attack and destroy – the convoy must be saved'. Self-tortured by the decision which he knew he must now make, the young captain gave the order, 'Fire depth charges'. Set to explode at varying depths of 150 and 300 feet, the charges catapulted from the thrower, ten in all. Seconds later in a succession of explosions which numbed the senses, the explosives erupted in great fountains of turbulent water rocketing high above the dark sea. Only those at some distance from the detonations survived the shock waves. The remainder died instantly with broken necks or from internal injuries. As *Northern Wave* approached it was seen there were many still in life-jackets who neither waved nor shouted but who gazed at them with sightless eyes, bobbing up and down in the swell of the Arctic sea.

The ill-luck which had dogged PQ14 from the beginning continued to manifest itself, for as the trawler ran on to begin rescue operations, engines were stopped and then rung 'full astern', but through a defect, could not be started again. In the engine room frantic efforts were made to correct the fault and to get the engine shaft turning. They were now drifting through the area where some men were still alive and as they neared a raft with six survivors aboard a line was thrown and held. However, the way was not off the ship and the raft, still attached, was swept under the stern beside the propellor. Knowing that at any moment the engines might start and the ship go astern with the certainty that the blades would cut them to pieces, the order was given to cast off. Unaware of the reason, the men on the raft could only stare in disbelief. The relief of being close to rescue turned to despair and anger as the ship moved further and further away.

But by now, the other trawler *Lord Middleton* had arrived and began to pick up survivors, dragging them barely conscious aboard. It was nearly ten minutes later that the engines of *Northern Wave* were restarted and because she had drifted some distance away another fifteen before she could return to commence rescue operations. A sea boat was sent away to pick up the more distant survivors but although the wreck was circled for a final search no further men were sighted and course was set to rejoin the convoy.

Aboard the two trawlers, everything possible was done to revive the rescued men. They were in extremely poor condition although still conscious. With wet clothes removed, they were wrapped in blankets and placed in the warmest compartments, and in an effort to restore circulation given brandy and whisky which made them sleepy. Barely five minutes later a signal to the trawlers from the medical officer of one of the accompanying destroyers warned the captains of both vessels on no account to give spirits to the survivors. It was too late. For those unfortunate men who fell asleep, it was a sleep from which there would be no awakening.*

Out of *Empire Howard*'s crew of fifty-four, only eighteen were rescued and of these nine died aboard the trawlers. As *Northern Wave* moved away, a periscope was sighted on the starboard bow only 400 yards distant and preparations were made to attack. On investigation however, the 'periscope' proved to be a small log from the wreckage floating upright. For a time the young captain searched the area carefully in the hope of finding some evidence of a submarine kill to justify the frightful decision he had made but there was nothing. Nothing except the slurping oil, the wreckage and the bobbing corpses in life jackets moving to the rhythm of the waves. With nine dead men aboard, a saddened and frustrated crew, the asdic-dome out of action and no hope of contacting the enemy, *Northern Wave* set off once more to join the convoy.

It had been a traumatic experience for Lieutenant Pardoe-Matthews and one which had been further aggravated by the failure of the ship's engines at a critical moment. Three days later, on arrival at the Kola inlet, he sent a report to the Senior British Naval Officer at Murmansk as follows.

. . . after careful consideration, I am of the opinion that had the *Northern Wave*'s engines been in proper condition for sea – all those picked up and probably more, would have been aboard the ship much earlier

* Although the giving of spirits would appear to have been the most natural thing to do, the loss of body heat from such exposure slowly produces a state of hypothermia. In this condition, the periphery blood vessels shut in an attempt to maintain the core temperature of the body. Intake of alcohol opens the blood vessels, forces the skin vessels to dilate and the blood, rushing into the cold surface tissues, is further chilled and on its return lowers the body core temperature still more. As a consequence, the temperature of the heart muscle drops, the fibres fail to contract normally and this in turn leads to cardiac failure.

with greater chance of survival. It is requested that recommendation be made to the proper quarter to avoid a re-occurrence of a similar regrettable incident.

But there were also bouquets. The master of the cargo ship SS *Briarwood* who had watched the vigorous manouevres of the destroyers around him, sent the following signal to the Naval Control Service Officer – Murmansk.

Considered opinion that I have never seen anything so keen and seamanlike as the destroyer *Bulldog* picking up torpedo tracks and turning completely around to contact the attacking U boats. My impression is that this action was instrumental in saving several ships in the convoy. I, Master of *Briarwood* submit this to my Lords of the Admiralty. Request information be passed through appropriate channels.

CHAPTER 2

The Merchant Navy Pays the Price

THE PENETRATION OF the destroyer screen and the subsequent sinking of *Empire Howard* was a matter of grave concern to Admiral Bonham-Carter. They were only halfway through their 2000 mile voyage and entering the most dangerous stretch between Bear Island and Murmansk. He became even more concerned when a signal was received from Admiralty, London informing him that intelligence sources in Norway had warned of enemy destroyers leaving the German naval base at Kirkenes, east of North Cape. Its purpose to engage and destroy the convoy.

To offset any threat from this direction, *Edinburgh* now took up a position ten miles ahead and a little to the south of the convoy. However, unknown to the admiral the destroyer attack had failed to materialise. The German flotilla much further south had encountered a force 9 gale with heavy snow. The sea washing over the decks froze every superstructure, covering the ships in a thick plating of ice. Binoculars, telescopes and gun sights were made useless. The guns were frozen solid and could not be fired, and the decks so slippery it became impossible to get a grip with seaboots. In the circumstances, the group commanding officer, Captain Alfred Schulze-Hinrichs, ordered his ships to return to base. This withdrawal was of course unknown to Admiral Bonham-Carter but it was at this point that a heaven-sent blessing arrived in the form of thick fog which hid the convoy, its escorts and *Edinburgh* from detection. The fog could not have come at a more fortunate time, for hardly had they entered the protective screen when about fourteen enemy planes arrived, with the clear intention of dealing with *Edinburgh* from the air prior to the proposed attack by their destroyer flotilla. Within the fog cover the cruiser circled at high speed taking refuge in the most concentrated mist banks. The aircraft were however not to be shaken off so easily. For over thirty minutes they criss-crossed and circled overhead looking for a gap to execute their dive-bombing attack, and from this it was assumed that the cruiser's presence was in part revealed by heat waves from the funnels disturbing the low fog bank. Fog, normally a maritime hazard, became in this area of naval warfare the convoy's friend.

Months later when a certain large convoy escorted by destroyers, heavy cruisers and a battleship were heading north in perfect visibility, the admiral despatched the signal – 'Chaplains of all Royal Naval ships will pray for fog'. Whether the Almighty was sufficiently awed by the author of the petition to grant the request we are not told.

As the evening of the 18th wore on, the intensity of the fog increased and thwarted in their attempts the aircraft called off the search. Two hours later the fog dispersed and on the following day in a force 9 gale *Edinburgh*, accompanied by the destroyers *Foresight* and *Forester*, left the convoy and arrived in the Kola inlet at 11 p.m. on Saturday 19 April. As *Edinburgh* made her way up stream guided by Russian pilots the temperature was now 10 degrees below freezing. Soon the intermittent sleet turned to snow with the flakes heaping where they fell. Masts and yardarms amplified by the flurries merged into white woolly trees. Cables and wires grew into fuzzy bands of cotton wool softening the outlines of their harsh functions. The snow fluttered silently down to pile up against the forward turrets and the massive superstructure. It brought an unnatural hush to upper deck activities as men picked their way across the white padded deck. Ice floes, stark against the black waters of the river floated by, thrust aside from their tidal course by the bows of the 10,000 ton cruiser.

There were a number of ships at anchor, all cargo vessels and obviously waiting to join the next convoy back to Iceland. But for some their stay would be indefinite. Barely afloat they had managed to limp into the Kola inlet. The scars, clear evidence of enemy action, were there for all to see. Gaping holes in the hulls, bows crumpled and rusting, distorted girders and stanchions that had once formed bridges. It would be many months perhaps years before they would be in a safe condition to return.

The anchorage opposite Vaenga was so deep it took most of the cruiser's cable before the heavy anchor reached the river bed. But they had arrived and apart from the tragedy of *Empire Howard*, safely. So far, fortune had favoured them yet in the days that followed during their brief stay, apprehension among the crew slowly built up as they faced the unwelcome prospect of the voyage home.

In considering all the factors surrounding the PQ14 convoy, Admiral Bonham-Carter was led to despatch the following signal to Admiralty, London.

Under present conditions with no hours of darkness, continually under air observation, submarines concentrating in the bottle necks, torpedo attacks to be expected, our destroyers unable to carry out a proper hunt or search owing to the oil situation, serious losses must be expected in every convoy. The remains of PQ14 were extremely lucky in the weather, in that when the first air attack developed, fog suddenly came down and though enemy bombers remained overhead for some time trying to sight *Edinburgh* and the convoy, they eventually had to leave.

I consider it was due to the fine work of the anti-submarine force that only one ship was lost, when several submarines were in the vicinity of the convoy. I wish to bring to the notice of their Lordships the name of the Commanding Officer of *Bulldog*, Commander M. Richmond who was Senior Officer of the close escort.

Until enemy aerodromes in North Norway are neutralized I consider convoys to North Russia should be suspended during the months of continuous light unless the very high percentage of losses can be accepted or sufficient air protection can be provided.

The admiral's report to the First Sea Lord, Admiral of the Fleet Sir Dudley Pound did not go unheeded. Admiral Pound fully recognised the obstacles to be overcome in sailing convoys to North Russia against increasing German attacks and the longer hours of daylight. He lost no time in expressing his concern to the Defence Committee, warning them that losses on the Arctic convoy route might become unacceptable. The change from a winter of constant darkness to a spring of constant daylight begged for a review of the circumstances governing the sailing of the convoys. Every twenty-four hours made it easier for German reconnaisance planes to locate the convoys and report back to their bases and this, allied to the build-up of U boats, aircraft and destroyers in North Norway, indicated that increased enemy attacks must be expected.

In response to the Commander-in-Chief, Sir John Tovey's appeal, additional numbers of destroyers and corvettes drawn from Western Approaches Command were promised to augment the Arctic convoy escorts. However, the return of so many damaged fully-laden ships from PQ14 convoy to Iceland, increasing the accumulation of supplies waiting to be shipped to North Russia, brought about relentless political pressure from the War Cabinet, led by Winston Churchill as Minister of Defence, for the size of the convoys to be increased rather than decreased. In part, this decision was influenced by Lord Beaverbrook's conviction that aid to the Russians was of the utmost importance. At the end of 1941, Churchill informed Stalin that he intended to provide a constant cycle of convoys leaving every ten days. The British offer no doubt contributed to Russian resistance in the defence of Moscow but its implementation provided Admiral Sir John Tovey with an almost impossible task. Enough ships to provide a sufficiently strong escort were simply not available. This was a direct reversal of Admiral Tovey's counsel, 'that if the convoys could not be delayed until the ice barrier receded to allow them to sail around the north of Bear Island, then they should be reduced in size'. Experience had also proved that in the event of gales convoys became scattered, making it impossible for escorts to protect them. But the Admiralty, having carefully analysed the situation, overruled Admiral Tovey's recommendation, deciding that future convoys were to be larger.

Time passed quickly during the nine days that *Edinburgh* lay at anchor in the deep waterway and her crew became involved in a variety of loading and unloading duties. This impression was brought about in part by the curious effect of perpetual daylight and by constant air raid alarms. Vaenga Bay lies a few miles below Murmansk on the eastern shore of the inlet. The port of Murmansk itself stands at the head of the river where cargoes of war materials were unloaded to aid the hard pressed Russian divisions with a front line only twenty miles away. With the opposing armies locked in deadly combat so near, Murmansk and ships in the inlet were exposed to incessant attacks by enemy bombers. Indeed it was anything but the restful time the crew had hoped for after the arduous voyage, throughout which they had been closed up at action stations for much of the time. Constant alarms triggered by so many U boat contacts had brought its toll of exhaustion and sleep now became the prime demand. But it was not to be.

The cruiser *Trinidad* lying damaged in dry dock at Rosta further up the river with a gaping hole in her side, claimed first priority. Not only did she urgently need the steel plates brought by *Edinburgh* but as most of the stores in the area where the torpedo had entered had been destroyed bundles of warm clothing and food were also desperately required. The day after *Edinburgh*'s arrival, two barges secured alongside. The steel plates were craned off, stored aboard and immediately taken up river to the waiting *Trinidad*. Much of the woollen clothing aboard *Edinburgh* had been donated by the British WVS and in view of *Trinidad*'s requirements *Edinburgh*'s supply staff were instructed to practically empty the fully stocked store. The following day, 20 April, a well loaded boat chugged its way up river and delivered the clothing to a thankful *Trinidad* crew. So far as food supplies were concerned the disabled cruiser was in a sorry state. The ship's company were trying to survive on a watery soup in which thin strips of Yak flesh had been dipped, and as a consequence *Edinburgh* generously consigned most of her potatoes and fresh food. The Russians could supply nothing. Since they had lost their granary – the Ukraine – very few crops had been grown in the USSR and the critical food situation appeared to be one of Hitler's premier weapons against his Russian adversary.

As one day followed another, each without sunrise or sunset, a steady stream of badly injured survivors from ships which had been torpedoed or dive-bombed in earlier convoys were brought aboard *Edinburgh*. All were stretcher cases, the worst of scores of mutilated seamen who by a miracle had survived impossible conditions in open boats. Often arms and legs deadened by frostbite had become gangrenous. The overcrowded Russian hospital did the best it could for them and where amputations had been necessary had carried them out but the operations themselves were unbelievably primitive. The Russians were not to be blamed. Scanty medical supplies were being rapidly exhausted by the demand of their own front line casualties. Hygiene at a minimum, amputated limbs developed gangrene and with remedial drugs often unobtainable the condition of many worsened.

And so they came aboard to be laid in rows in the spare aircraft hangar waiting to be brought back to the United Kingdom, in the meantime receiving whatever immediate aid could be given from the cruiser's own medical officers. Through the eyes of most there shone a light of hope – a will to live – a deep faith that now they were aboard a British ship things would be all right despite their condition. In others that hope had died. Dull lifeless faces disclosed the message as surely as if it had been spoken. Some with severe amputations still gangrenous had little wish to live, only a fatalistic attitude that even if they succeeded in reaching Britain, and there was no certainty about that, there would be no satisfaction in existing as trunkated bodies to be fed and tended for the rest of their days.

Each had a story to tell. A story of miraculous survival from every Arctic condition and circumstance that the mind could imagine and from all the ravage and destruction the enemy could hurl at them. From most of these accounts there shone that light of courage, of resolution, of fortitude, which matching other chronicles in our island history became submerged and finally lost in the publicity of graver national issues. There was the story told by the captain of a cargo vessel torpedoed near the Great Ice Barrier. In his own words he described what happened.

The torpedo struck us on the port side in the engine room. There was a loud explosion as the water was thrown up. I was in the chart room at the time and rushed on to the bridge. Looking aft I saw that the port motor boat was hanging in two pieces from the davits. I noticed a large number of men on the after boat deck, including gunners, firemen and sailors. They were endeavouring to lower the only remaining lifeboat. They had just succeeded in bringing the boat to the water line with a number of men in it when a second torpedo struck the ship on the starboard side. The men in the lifeboat and those on the boat deck were all killed by flying debris. After giving order to abandon ship the officers lowered my small dinghy and I collected my brief case and made my way to it. I found several of the officers already in the dinghy along with some of the crew and discovered there were 13 people in her. Unfortunately the boat then fouled the wreckage of the motor boat, which upset the dinghy, throwing all the occupants into the water. The Second and Third Officers managed to grab the lifelines hanging from the deck and regain the ship. The Chief Officer who had his duffel coat on was floating but unable to swim owing to water collecting in the sleeves and hood of his coat. I heard him shouting for help but owing to the weight of my case on my back and the freezing water it was all I could do to keep myself afloat and struggle to the upturned boat. Several members of the crew had got away on 4 rafts and some clinging to the dinghy managed to swim to one of these rafts. A few minutes later a third torpedo struck the ship penetrating the hold where the explosives were stored. There was an enormous explosion amidships and when the smoke and debris had cleared I saw that the ship had broken in two and in a second or two she disappeared.

One of the Transport Officers swam over to the upturned dinghy and together we climbed on to the keel and tried to right it. We managed to roll the boat over but she came too far and capsized again. We tried a second time and this time managed to right the boat which was by now about one foot under water. We stood on the forward end and a few feet of the after end lifted out of the water. I emptied my brief case and used it as a bailer and after a struggle managed to reduce the water level in the boat and we climbed in. We rowed amongst the wreckage and picked up one of the signalmen. A few minutes later a submarine broke surface while the periscope of another sub was sighted at some distance. The submarine came alongside one of the rafts and a seaman was taken aboard and asked the ship's name. Having given the information he was handed a bottle of water and some bread and after taking a photograph of the survivors on the raft the submarine captain told them the course and the distance to North Russia.

It was very cold in the boat as the water was at a temperature of 0 degrees centigrade and all the survivors were wet through. Whilst rowing around I came across the upturned lifeboat but decided it was impossible to attempt to right it without assistance from the men on the rafts. I told all rafts to paddle over towards the lifeboat but when they arrived they were too cold and numb to do anything about it. One man with his brains knocked out died on the raft so I buried him. The Second Engineer also died from injuries received on board and he was also buried. Some time later a ship was sighted on the horizon. We burnt flares to attract her attention and at midnight HMS *Lotus* came over and picked us up and two days later we arrived in North Russia, most of us suffering from intense frostbite in the feet and legs.

There were several members of my crew who played an heroic part in this tragedy. The Chief Steward remained behind after the ship was abandoned although he heard the order, attending to the injured. He further assisted in rescuing the Second Engineer from the engine room and having put him on a stretcher carried him on to the raft. Whilst doing this the third torpedo struck and the Chief Steward went down with the ship but managed to swim to the raft. The Second Cook also stayed behind and assisted in the rescue of the Second Engineer. After completing this rescue he went round the ship distributing lifejackets to other members of the crew who had lost theirs but when the third torpedo struck he was killed by falling debris and went down with the ship.

My Chief Engineer also behaved magnificently, firstly in leading the rescue party to the Second Engineer who was trapped in the engine room in spite of knowing that the order had been given to abandon ship. Although badly injured in the leg he carried on with the rescue work showing great bravery and finally only just managed to get away from the ship in time. The rescued Second Engineer had already been on three trips to Russia with me and volunteered for this fourth trip. This time he was not so fortunate and was trapped in the engine room as the two torpedoes struck, one from either side. Although badly injured in the legs and spine, with the aid of the rescuers he was hauled up and put on to one of the rafts but as the third torpedo struck he was blown into the sea. He managed to cling to some wreckage and was eventually pulled back on to the raft where he died from his injuries and exposure. Outstanding courage was shown by the Senior Wireless Operator also who despite the order to abandon ship succeeded in getting his messages away and remained at his station until satisfied that the messages had got through. I'm glad to say he managed to get away on one of the rafts.

There was the story given by another captain who survived the torpedoeing of his ship when 39 of his crew of 59 lost their lives.

We had been repeatedly attacked by enemy aircraft and I made a course for the north east which brought us up against the ice barrier and by taking cover in the fog banks managed to avoid being spotted by other aircraft searching for us. Later the weather cleared. The sea was fairly rough and at about 4 p.m. that day we were hit by a torpedo on the port side under the bridge. As I rushed out on to the bridge I was struck by falling debris and was unconscious for a few minutes. Just as I came round I heard another explosion as a second torpedo plunged into the engine room. The port boat which was in the process of being lowered was blown away. About one minute later there was a third explosion in the after end of the vessel. I think the ammunition store in the after hold must have exploded as I saw a great column of smoke rising and could smell cordite. The ship immediately broke into three pieces; the main mast crashed down and one man who was lowering the forward fall of the lifeboat was blown away and the boat left hanging by the after fall. The explosion also destroyed the starboard lifeboat. Three rafts were managed to be released from the ship and I threw a knife to one of the crew and told him to cut the after fall of the hanging lifeboat. This boat then crashed into the sea and immediately became waterlogged. I gave the order to abandon ship by which time there was only one man left on board with me and we both jumped into the sea. The bridge was then about 5 feet above the water and one minute later the vessel disappeared. I swam with this sailor to the waterlogged boat where there was already one man and having climbed in we found that water was up above our waists. We picked up several other members of the crew and finally there were 17 of us in this waterlogged lifeboat. Before the fog shut down visibility altogether I saw 7 men on one raft and 14 on another. We did everything possible to get the boat cleared of water which at the time was 0 degrees centigrade but the crew became extremely cold and numb. Four men died during the first five hours and we were unable to do anything for them. I took the lifejackets off their bodies and buried them. Some time later the weather moderated and the fog lifted. We found a bucket and with this and the pump we managed to get the water down to the level of the buoyancy tanks. One by one the men died from exposure and shock until there were only four of us left alive. About this time a large submarine surfaced with *U13* painted in black on the side of the conning tower and round this number was painted a black horseshoe. Forward of the conning tower was a 3-inch gun. The U boat closed into my boat and its commander asked me if the ship's captain was a survivor and I told him 'No', as there was the distinct likelihood they would take me prisoner. The submarine then went over to the raft and the men on it were asked the same question to which they replied that they thought the ship's captain had gone down with the vessel. The U boat commander then spoke to my Chief Officer and was asked if he was a Bolshevik and on learning that he was not said, 'Then what the hell are you going to Russia for?' The Chief Officer was then given the course and distance to Nova Zembla, also a bottle of wine, another of gin and five loaves of black bread. The sub had a machine gun trained on us during the conversation and was taking cine-photographs of the men on the rafts as they were receiving the food, etc. The submarine commander who was about 6 ft tall and with a red beard, spoke English fluently and was dressed in an ordinary peak cap and a coat similar to our duffel coats. After about five minutes the submarine submerged and moved off. We rigged the sail and steered a course to the south-east and towards land which I estimated about 20 miles distant. Early the next morning I gave the crew some pemmican and a small tot of brandy each. Pemmican is stored in most lifeboats and is a preparation of lean flesh-meat, dried and pounded, mixed with fat and other ingredients. Later, we picked up 9 men from one of the rafts and at about 10 o'clock that night with 13 men in the boat we landed on a small island off the coast of Nova Zembla. We found the island unin-habited so on landing we rigged our sail as a tent, lighted a fire and made some pemmican soup to warm us. We found a number of birds eggs which we put into the soup and despite the eggs containing young birds it tasted good. We rested for two days and then climbing some high ground we sighted a vessel which appeared to be stopped. We launched our boat and sailed towards this ship which proved to be American and was aground. Having boarded her we found 7 men from one of our rafts already aboard thus making a total of 20 survivors from our vessel. We remained on board and a week later a Russian survey ship arrived which brought us back to North Russia.

And the story like that of the cargo vessel *Induna* which had been torpedoed near the ice-field. At that time they were about 175 miles from land, fully exposed to sub-zero temperatures in an open boat and subject to gales and snow storms without warning. Loaded with 32 instead of a maximum capacity of 25, they were grossly overcrowded. Not only were the men unable to take exercise to keep warm but attempts to row were hampered. The boat itself was leaking badly and with the sea breaking in over the side required constant baling with buckets to check the rising water level. In the boat in charge was the ship's mate, a Mr Rowland. A sober assessment of the situation gave him little ground for optimism. In his own mind, he had to admit it would be a race against time. How long could their bodies hold out against exposure to the wet and the cold before they were rescued? To the men he presented a cheerful and optimistic picture of their chances; they had food and water and the following wind if assisted by sailing and rowing would help them on towards land. The men seated on the thwarts were the most fortunate for the exercise of rowing kept the blood circulating. It was sheer hell for the rest. The injured lay on the bottom boards in freezing water. One of these was the donkeyman, whose job on the ship had been to operate the steam winch. He had been severely burned and was in great pain; every jolt of the pitching boat added to his torture. Others sat propped against the sides or perched together in the bows, while the rest bunched themselves in the stern sheets. In this manner, the small band of survivors set out on their long haul to Russia on the morning of 30 March 1942. Although the boat was running before the wind the men rowed in spells to keep as warm as possible. But when night fell it grew much colder and hands became too numb to grasp the oars. In the boat's lockers were seven bottles of whisky and these were passed around to combat the cold with a warning to drink only sparingly. Unfortunately some of the men drank a great deal of the spirit and becoming drowsy fell asleep, some into too deep a sleep. As the grey streaks of dawn appeared, those who had survived the night roused themselves to face the next day. It was soon discovered that not only had the donkeyman slipped mercifully out of this life but six of the older seamen who had drunk deeply the night before were lying frozen and stiff and would never wake again. With the chill awareness that any one of them could suffer the same fate in the hours ahead, the men lifted the bodies of their shipmates over the side and saw them float away, leaving each man alone with his thoughts.

All that day they sailed on, occasionally assisting their progress with ever-weakening attempts to hold and pull the oars. The insidious effects of frostbite were undermining their efforts. None of the men were wearing sea boots. There had been no time to gather such things between the torpedo explosion and the sinking of the ship, which meant that their feet and ankles were in water all the time. The foresail was unlashed and rigged as a shield against the wind and water on the weather side of the boat and although they were not hungry everyone ate a few biscuits. They were all desperately thirsty. The water in their containers was frozen into solid blocks. The only way to get at it was to break open the can and as there was no way of melting the blocks, suck the cracked-off lumps. Even the pemmican among the stored food was frozen into unmanageable masses. Like the water it had to be hacked with knives, not an easy task with frozen hands.

That evening, with the sharp lesson of the previous night very much in mind, the men took only a small sip of the whisky before settling down for the night. In the misery and discomfort of swirling snow and biting wind, they felt the cold penetrating deeper and deeper. Early the following morning, Wednesday 1 April, Mr Rowland's roll-call revealed that two more had died during the night. It was only with the greatest difficulty that the bodies could be lifted and placed into the water. As the day developed the crew looked out over the turbulent water with growing despair, wondering how much longer their bodies could withstand such exposure. From the original 32, their number was reduced to 23. While the mate Mr Rowland steered, the rest huddled together as best they could. In this way they could get some shelter from the wind and some mutual warmth from one another. Some of the men's legs had become so numb they were unable to move without assistance. During the afternoon one of the greasers slumped over his oar and then rolled into the bottom of the boat. An hour later a steward, one of the four men in the bows, slid forward into a coma from which there would be no recovery. These two had to be left where they had fallen, as by now no one had the strength to lift their bodies over the side.

As dawn of the fourth day broke, any hopes of seeing a coast line were dashed by the sight of the unbroken monotony of a heaving grey sea. Four more men had lost the fight for survival during the night and only seventeen remained alive. As the hours of daylight passed and early evening approached with the prospect of another cold remorseless night, the last few shreds of hope were slowly ebbing away. Just before six o'clock with the evening light upon them, one of the crew in the stern thought he saw an object in the far distance and pointing south, mumbled something about a ship.. All eyes scanned the dim horizon in the failing light and indeed there was something there. The mate using his binoculars with trembling hands, studied the object with all the presence of mind he could muster. The others watched him with quickening pulses. It was impossible to identify at first for it was at least five miles away but it was certainly not a ship. Suddenly it dawned on Mr Rowland what it actually was. In a voice trembling with emotion he turned to the others and said, 'Lads we've made it – it's a lighthouse'. In fact it was Cape Sviatoi lighthouse on the eastern shore of the Kola inlet. Even in their extreme weakness they managed to reach out and clasp one another's hands. Too exhausted to cheer, the men wept openly. The adrenalin of hope ran through their veins like fire – they were going to be all right. Within minutes they heard the sound of planes approaching low over the water. Soon three Russian fighters were clearly visible and they flew around the boat several times. After acknowledging the flag the crew displayed, the fighters flew back to the coast to bring help. At eight o'clock, just two hours later, a Russian minesweeper came alongside to take them aboard. Their numbed and swollen legs gave the rescued men no power to stand. The earlier exhilaration had drained the little strength remaining and left them frozen effigies of living beings. In this helpless state they could not get themselves out of the boat. The Russians had to come aboard to fasten ropes and hoist them on to the ship. One by one they were carried into a warm compartment, stripped, then wrapped in thick woollen coats and given hot coffee to drink.

The minesweeper after setting course for Murmansk had made a small detour towards the east during the night. While the survivors on the *Induna* slept, the Russians came across another boat of survivors; this turned out to be the *Induna*'s port lifeboat. There were only nine left alive – the two anti-aircraft gunners, five Americans, a fireman and a steward's boy, all were in a desperate condition. Shortly after reaching Murmansk on 3 April, one of the Americans and the boy died in hospital.

From the *Induna*'s total number of 66 men, only 24 survived. After weeks of treatment six of these were able to walk and were later sent to England. Many of those kept in hospital at Murmansk had such severe frostbite that they had to have feet or legs amputated.

Then there were stories like that of the bosun of the *Empire Ranger* and the cabin boy. After being dive-bombed, the ship sank quickly and only one lifeboat managed to get away. Thirty-eight, including a fourteen year-old cabin boy were packed into this boat. For six days they were carried along by wind and tide, subjected to snowstorms, gales and the freezing wind. Each day took its toll. A Russian tug eventually found them drifting not far from the coast. Half propped up in the bows sat an elderly seaman, his beard white with snow and frost looking out across the tumbling sea, frozen into immobility, quite dead. In the boat huddled together were the frozen bodies of 35 men. Another two were found to be still alive. One was the cabin boy, David, a Scot from the city of Edinburgh. Stretched across him providing warmth and protecting him from the snow and wind lay the bosun, more dead than alive. Although the boy's feet were in a dreadful state from frostbite through long immersion in ice-cold water in the boat he eventually recovered. But for the bosun the bid to save the boy's life extracted a terrible penalty. The Russian hospital into which he was later admitted found that to save his life it was necessary to amputate both arms and legs.

The bosun revealed later that on the fifth day of their ill-fated voyage, when only four or five men remained alive, fate played an almost unbelievable last cruel trick. A swirling mist had descended on them fanned by a bitter breeze. As the fog thickened it blanketed visibility altogether shutting out all sound. Only the ceaseless lapping of water against the boat could be heard. Then suddenly they heard a whistle. The sound faded then rose again, louder and more constant. Hearts raced with excitement. Surely it was someone from a rescue boat trying to locate them. With what little strength was left they tried to shout but despite their efforts there was no answer. Still the whistle persisted. First it seemed to be ahead and then astern, the sound was eerie, almost supernatural. In their low state of mind, the mystery deepening every minute became almost frightening. Desperate and frustrated, their eyes tried to pierce the fog bank but found nothing. Minutes later, their hopes came tumbling when the riddle was solved. On the thwart, gently rolling with the movement of the sea lay an empty bottle. As the wind swept through the boat it played on the open end of the bottle trilling the whistling sound. As the bosun said later, it was a time when hope turned to despair, optimism to despondency, the worst moment of their ordeal.

CHAPTER 3

The Loading of the Gold Bullion

As EACH DAY PASSED and more casualties arrived aboard the cruiser, the vast hangar took on the appearance of a hospital ward and the small sick bay, an emergency operating theatre. Day and night, Surgeon-Commander W. F. Lascelles, RNVR, Surgeon-Lieutenant D. C. Lillie, MB, ChB, RNVR, Surgeon-Lieutenant L. Cama, RNVR, and Surgeon-Lieutenant (D.) J. K. Donald, RNVR, worked ceaselessly, operating on the wounded seamen. In many cases they found that wounds had become septic and amputations of feet and legs were necessary to save life. That section of the ship and those involved became caught up in a war apart. Surgically, it was a question of saving as much as possible of a man.

The time was approaching when *Edinburgh* would leave the Kola inlet for home. But two days before she sailed an event occurred which proved to be rare in the many tasks which the Royal Navy are called upon to perform. Supply Petty Officer Arthur Start described in his own words what happened.

I had been asleep for about an hour when I was awakened by the bugler sounding off, 'Both watches of the duty hands fall in, in the starboard waist'. My messmate sat up with a start, looked at his watch and said – 'What the 'ells going on – it's quarter to bloody midnight'. When we arrived on deck we could hardly believe our eyes. The scene was like something from a film. Secured along the starboard side were two barges

53

and at vantage points aboard were about a score of Russian soldiers armed with 'Tommy' guns held at the ready. On our own ship, stationed at regular intervals from the deck and up ladders to the flight deck were also our own Royal Marines keeping guard. As we watched, a tarpaulin covering the barge's cargo was drawn back to reveal scores of ammunition boxes. The natural assumption at first was that these contained small arms ammunition – but why should there be such security for a routine job of work? And then in a matter of minutes the truth was out. The boxes contained not ammunition but gold – gold bullion. Over five tons of it to be stored in the cruiser and shipped to the United Kingdom. The boxes, rope handled, were extremely heavy, each needing two men to lift them. In the dull grey daylight of the Arctic midnight we carried those boxes all the way up to the flight deck and there lowered them by ropes through a shaft trunking to the bomb room three decks below. All the time we were unloading the gold there seemed to be an aura of evil present. An uncomfortable feeling of impending disaster. We all felt it – most expressed it. Superstition is a strong characteristic with sailors throughout the world. The ominous feeling persisted and when part way through the operation, sleet started falling and the heavy red stencilling on the boxes ran freely to drip a trail of scarlet along the snow-covered decks, apprehension redoubled. One seaman expressed the thoughts of all of us when passing an officer he said, 'It's going to be a bad trip, sir, this is Russian gold dripping with blood!' They were prophetic words indeed.

The value of the gold taken aboard *Edinburgh* was estimated then to be in the order of about £5 million. The current value is thought to be nearer £45 million. The bullion was in fact, part of a deal between the Russian Government and the United States Treasury, a down-payment on thousands of tons of war equipment for the Red Army fighting the bitter war against the Nazi invaders attacking Moscow and Stalingrad. Little did the Edinburgh crew know that the gold had its own history of death and blood. The 12-inch long ingots were believed to have been part of the stockpile of bullion accumulated by the Czar in the days prior to the Russian Revolution, which broke out in March 1917. The transportation of the gold from Moscow to the port of Murmansk was in itself a daring and hazardous operation. The 1000 mile long single line rail track running north from the capital passed, in some places, no more than 50 miles from the Finnish and German armies, against whom the Russians were fighting a bitter and courageous battle to preserve their lifeline of supplies to and from the north. No doubt the enemy would have been highly delighted to have captured such a valuable prize. Now it was being stacked in the bomb room, a specially armoured compartment of the ship used for high-risk cargo, especially high explosive ammunition, deep in the bowels. There it lay, a king's ransom, over five tons of pure gold, stacked in boxes neatly piled against the steel bulkheads in this strong room not more than 20 feet square.

The day before Edinburgh left the Kola inlet, the lower deck was cleared and Captain Faulkner announced to the ship's company some of the details of the imminent convoy QP11 returning to Iceland which the cruiser would escort. On Tuesday morning, 28 April, the convoy of 13 ships sailed in single line down the inlet. Seven were British: Briarwood, Dan-y-Bryn, Trehatta, Athol Templar, Gallant Fox, Ballot and the Dunboyne. Five were American: West Cheswald, Stone Street, El Dina, El Estra and the Moomadmer; and there was one Russian, the Ciolkovsky. Close astern came the destroyer escort and HMS Edinburgh flying the flag of Admiral Bonham-Carter. From the distant cape to the west, now in possession of the Germans, observers watched the little convoy sail off and at once reported back to German Naval

Command – Norway. From that moment the wheels were set in motion to attack and destroy the westward bound convoy.

The German Naval Command's excursions into the Arctic Ocean to attack convoys were limited by reason of ever decreasing supplies of oil fuel. One of Hitler's objectives in attacking Russia was to acquire the Caucasian oilfields to maintain his vast war machine. When the winter battle before Moscow destroyed these hopes the Rumanian oilfields remained his only source of supply. His vast war machine with the extended lines of communication into Russia now demanded more than the Rumanian oilfields could produce. He had anticipated that by the winter of 1941–42 he would have gained control of the Caucasian oilfields to supplement his supplies but the dogged resistance of the Russian armies before Moscow prevented him reaching this source and his planned campaign had to be drastically reduced. The rationing of oil fuel fell most heavily on the navy as priority had to be given to tanks and planes. By April 1942, delivery had been reduced from 46,000 tons to 8000 tons and in the light of this critical situation German Navy Group North issued the following restrictive order, 'All operations to be discontinued including those by light forces. The sole exceptions are operations made necessary by enemy action'. From now on, any naval engagement was guided purely by the importance of the operation; where the chances of success justified the cost in fuel. But when the 'Admiral Arctic' – Admiral Hubert Schmundt at the German naval port of Kirkenes in North Norway – was given authority to dispatch three of his heavily armed destroyers into the Barents Sea to attack the QP11 convoy, it seemed a miracle. In addition to the destroyer group, Admiral Schmundt alerted seven of his U boats in the northern area to close in on QP11 in support of his surface vessels.

By the afternoon of the convoy's departure, QP11 had cleared the inlet and formed convoy position heading due north.

The escort was made up of six British destroyers:

Bulldog, Commander Maxwell Richmond, DSO, MBE, RN

Beagle, Commander Roger Medley, RN

Foresight, Commander Jocelyn Stuart Salter, RN

Forester, Lieut-Commander George Huddart, RN

Amazon, Lieut-Commander Lord Teynham, RN

Beverley, Lieutenant Rodney Athelstan Price, RN

Four corvettes:

Oxlip, Lieut-Commander Alfred Creighton Collinson, RN

Saxafrage, Lieut-Commander Edmund Chapman, RN

Camanula, Lieut-Commander Alfred Hine, RN

Snowflake, Lieut-Commander Sidney Cuthbertson, RN, and two Russian destroyers.

With them was the armed trawler *Lord Middleton*, Lieutenant P. Jameson, RNR, which had the responsibility of picking up survivors should the need arise. For the first 300 miles the four British minesweepers *Harrier, Hussar, Niger* and *Gossamer* also escorted them and then, their work done, returned to base at Murmansk.

The close escort force commanded by Commander Richmond was quite adequate to deal with U boat attacks which were expected but none of the escort vessels was sufficiently armed to successfully repulse heavy air attack and neither were they capable of engaging the large, heavily armed Narvik-class destroyers on anything like equal terms. However, *Edinburgh* was certainly expected to match any destroyer attack which might be mounted. Bristling with guns, her radar searching the sea and sky and the asdic pinging the depths for intruding U boats, the heavy cruiser, protective, watchful, steamed patiently along astern of the

six-knot convoy, with her vast fortune of shining gold.
Asdic was a machine operated from the bottom of the ship
to detect submarines under water. It was an echo-sounding
device that transmitted a signal into the depths which
rebounded from an object such as a U boat, giving the
approximate position. The initials ASDIC stood for 'Anti-
Submarine Detection Investigation Committee', set up
between the two world wars to combat submarine warfare.

By 3 o'clock that afternoon the thin strip of coastline had
disappeared leaving only a great world of water. Later, the
wind from the north-east brought its customary snow
storms and with it a turbulent sea. It made things difficult
for the empty merchant ships pitching and tossing in the
long troughs. With no stabilising weight against the impact
of waves the vessels rolled and staggered to the crests,
propellers half out of water thrashing violently in the surf.

Every so often, one of the escorts would steam up
through the line of ships, shepherding a stray back into line
or encouraging a slowing vessel to pick up speed. It was
equally uncomfortable for the escorts themselves who
wallowed and rolled in the heaving sea. Conditions below
decks were chaotic. Everything became wet through. Water
poured down ventilator shafts and companion ways.
Flooded messdecks were crowded areas of saturated clothes,
broken china, pots and pans and lashed hammocks that had
broken away from stowage racks. Men were sea-sick over
everything. With cooking arrangements impossible, it was
tea and corned beef sandwiches every meal time or when it
could be snatched.

At 8 o'clock on Wednesday morning the 29th, the enemy
found them. It was a Junkers 88 reconnaisance plane. Sitting
on the horizon, it circled endlessly, transmitting homing
messages to its base reporting speed, course and consti-
tution of the convoy. Bridge personnel and look-outs
watched helplessly as the aircraft flew up and down across
the distant rim of sea. Smug, unreachable, unassailable, it

was the eyes of the enemy, and the crew hating the sight of the predator could only stand at their action stations and hurl curses at it.

The presence of the reconnaisance plane was a matter of concern for Admiral Bonham-Carter. Spotter planes were ever a feature of the convoy run through the Barents Sea but to be detected at such an early stage in the voyage augured ill. It meant that enemy attacks in one form or another could soon be expected. But for Admiral Schmundt in Norway, the incoming reports gave immense satisfaction for it confirmed his conviction that a planned raid by his forces was justified. He now had two objectives. The destruction of the convoy and the elimination of the big fat prize accompanying it – the cruiser *Edinburgh*. Aware that QP11 was proceeding steadily north he knew that it was only a matter of hours before that course would be changed. It would soon meet the ice barrier and have to turn westward. His policy was also governed by the fuel situation. He had no intention of chasing all over the Arctic after the British vessels. Rather he would let them come to him. He therefore ordered his destroyer group of three to be ready to put to sea. These were the *Hermann Schoemann*, Lieut-Commander Heinrich Wittig; *Z24*, Lieut-Commander Martin Salzwedel, and *Z25*, Lieut-Commander Heinz Peters, all belonging to Destroyer Group Arctic under Captain Schulze-Hinrichs. After alerting the new force of torpedo-carrying aircraft and instructing his U boats to take up position across the estimated path of the convoy, he waited.

In the hours that followed, the convoy with *Edinburgh* in attendance was constantly employed in altering course to avoid icefields and on Thursday morning frequent sightings of U boats brought about further course alterations with destroyer escorts speeding around depth-charging the enemy. With the constant presence of U boats it was no place for a large cruiser to be plodding along at the 6 knot speed set by the cargo vessels. The admiral ordered Captain

Faulkner to take the cruiser some 20 miles ahead and to adopt a zig-zag course to avoid possible U boat attacks. This order was immediately put into force and after signalling *Bulldog* of her intention, *Edinburgh* sped away until she was lost out of sight over the horizon. The decision was undoubtedly a wise one but observers in the cruiser and in some of the escort ships were puzzled why she had not detached one of the destroyers as escort to provide a screen for her, particularly with U boats popping up in all directions. An officer in one of the accompanying destroyers who watched *Edinburgh*'s departure considered at the time that the cruiser was tactically wrong to go out ahead without taking one of the destroyers with her. Left alone with the convoy, Commander Richmond must have been well aware of the added responsibility now placed upon his shoulders. While his group of small destroyers and corvettes fitted with aging depth charge equipment and guns could cope with enemy submarines, they would be no match for large German destroyers with guns equal in fire power to *Edinburgh*'s, should they come upon them. The enemy's base at Kirkenes was not all that distance away and Richmond was well aware that an attack by these ships could occur at any time.

And while there was some consolation in the knowledge that *Edinburgh* was somewhere ahead protecting the convoy's advance, there was no certainty that the enemy would approach from that direction. An attack might well be mounted from astern or from the south supported by aircraft. In this tense atmosphere the convoy steamed sluggishly homeward.

It was some time later at the end of her 20-mile patrol amid intermittent snow showers that disaster overtook *Edinburgh*. The time 4 p.m. Waiting submerged in the path of the cruiser lay U boat *456* commanded by Lieutenant Max Teichert. As he brought his periscope to bear the first thing he saw was not the crop of mastheads of the convoy he expected but the bulk of a large unaccompanied cruiser, the *Edinburgh*. At first he could hardly trust his eyes. Almost in disbelief his periscope swept the horizon in every direction. There was not an escort vessel in sight. It was not an opportunity to be missed and in mounting excitement Teichert decided to take full advantage of the situation. He noticed that the cruiser was zig-zagging, not at the 33 knots she was capable of to avoid torpedoes but at a leisurely 19 knots. By careful observation he tried to estimate the complex zig-zag pattern employed by the cruiser. Quite soon she was well within firing range and with a last minute check he saw the ship turn on to a new leg of her course which he estimated she would probably maintain for some minutes. He dare not miss for his stock of torpedoes had been reduced to two. With a final check on speed, course and range, Teichert gave the order, 'Fire one', and a few seconds later, 'Fire two'. The expected muffled vibrations rippled through the hull as the torpedoes left the tubes, speeding on course with their deadly warheads towards the unsuspecting *Edinburgh*.

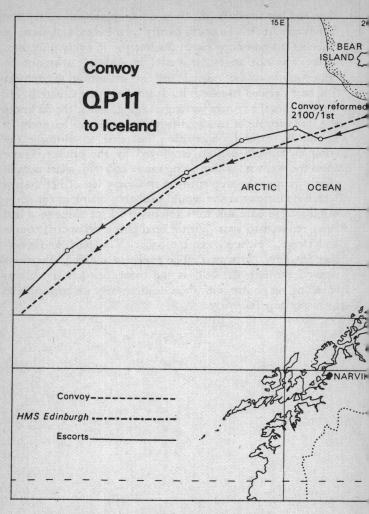

Convoy

QP 11
to Iceland

15 E

BEAR ISLAND

Convoy reformed 2100/1st

ARCTIC OCEAN

NARVIK

Convoy------------
HMS Edinburgh -----·-----·-----·
Escorts_____

Sequence of events from *Edinburgh*'s departure from
the Kola inlet on 28 April 1942 to her sinking on 2 May.

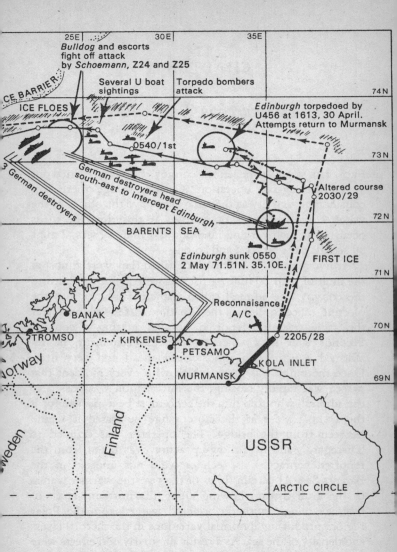

25E 30E 35E

Bulldog and escorts
fight off attack
by *Schoemann*, Z24 and Z25

ICE BARRIER

Several U boat
sightings

Torpedo bombers
attack

ICE FLOES

74N

Edinburgh torpedoed by
U456 at 1613, 30 April.
Attempts return to Murmansk

0540/1st

3 German destroyers

73N

German destroyers head
south-east to intercept *Edinburgh*

Altered course
2030/29

72N

BARENTS SEA

Edinburgh sunk 0550
2 May 71.51N. 35.10E.

FIRST ICE

71N

BANAK

Reconnaisance
A/C

TROMSO

KIRKENES

2205/28

Norway

PETSAMO

KOLA INLET

MURMANSK

69N

Sweden

Finland

USSR

ARCTIC CIRCLE

CHAPTER 4

Edinburgh is Torpedoed

FROM THE MOMENT she left the convoy, *Edinburgh* carried out a planned zig-zag operation. On the bridge there was considerable activity as the radar plot gave the officer of the watch correct changes of course. At this time the turns occurred at such varying intervals as 1 min. 20 secs, 2 mins 30 secs, 0 mins 50 secs, and so on.

At five minutes to four o'clock when they were almost at the limit of their 20 mile patrol and were about to return to the convoy, the admiral called Captain Faulkner into the plotting office to discuss the situation. A few minutes later the asdic operator reported he was getting a contact. Seconds later in a voice tense with excitement, he re-affirmed a firm echo almost dead ahead and very near. Once the range was given which with every moment that passed was rapidly closing, the information was passed to the admiral, who told him the echo must be a mistake for if the U boat were at the close range he stated it would be seen from the bridge. The operator was ordered to 'Disregard', and no follow-up action was taken from the reported contact. False echoes were not unusual in the Barents Sea. At certain times of the year the warmer waters of the Gulf Stream flowing along the northern coast of Norway mingle with the ice-cold waters from the Polar region, producing abnormal variations in the thermal layers and density of the sea. As a result singularly odd effects were often produced on asdic screens. But in this case the young operator had made no mistake. The firm strong echo was indeed a U boat, the German submarine *U456*. And *Edinburgh*, unaware of impending disaster, sailed on.

Within the cruiser, normal routine was being followed to the letter. The pipe had just sounded, 'Fall out from action stations' and 'Non-duty hands to tea'. Most of the crew had been at 'Stand by action stations' for the last 48 hours. This was the earliest opportunity for some to relax in the comparative comfort of their own messdecks. For the first time since the ship had left Murmansk, the pipe, heard throughout the ship including by those at their sea-going stations, seemed to dispense an atmosphere of relaxation. There was a natural buoyant air of optimism, a sense of security. It was in this unguarded moment that no one, not even the bridge look-outs, saw the tell-tale silver wakes of the deadly steel fish streaking through the Arctic waters towards the ship. Both were on target. As they plunged into the cruiser on the starboard side there were two enormous explosions. The first torpedo, amidships, ploughed through to the region of the forward boiler room and below the stoker's messdeck, destroying compartments through to the port side, killing all personnel in the blast area and flooding other compartments in a deluge of oil and water. The second struck aft, ripping off the stern, blowing the whole quarter deck upwards like a sheet of paper, and wrapped itself around the guns of 'Y' turret with the barrels protruding through the steel decking. With it went the rudder and two of the four propellor shafts. So great was the explosion that it blasted the bottom plates of the ship downwards to form a distorted fin or rudder. With a noise of rending metal and the dreadful thunder of tons of sea water flooding through under enormous pressure, the cruiser shuddered to a stop listing heavily to starboard. The proud warship, once the envy of cruiser squadrons, had in five seconds become a grotesque coffin of steel and smashed bodies, with two enormous gaping wounds lapped by the cold grey sea.

In compartments and gangways just above the explosion areas men stumbled and staggered in the darkness, cannoning into one another as they made for the exits, cursing violently when they could not be found. The two torpedoes had destroyed all electrical power to the gun turrets and only one of the forward turrets, 'B' turret, could be operated at all. Such was the damage to the engine rooms and the stern that only limited power could be applied to move the ship forward. At that moment, if Teichert had had one more torpedo he could have applied the *coup de grâce*. But as it was he could only submerge and wait.

Below the cruiser's decks, conditions where the first torpedo had struck were chaotic. For the few who survived there it was a nightmare of living hell. Leading Stoker Leonard Bradley described the scene.

Just before the torpedo struck I happened to go into the stokers' messdeck which was fairly crowded at the time and was talking to a friend of mine, a young amateur boxer called Harrington. As we chatted, the torpedo exploded in the oil tank below us. The whole messdeck split in two and as the lights went out Harrington and I and at least another 50 men fell straight through into the storage tank which was partially filled. The emergency lighting failed to come on and we were down there in complete darkness, floundering around in oil and water. In the blackness with men around screaming and shouting, I managed at last to get a footing and started to make my way towards where I thought the hatch might be.

As I moved, I heard Taff Harrington near me. I called out 'Taff', and he grabbed me. The oil was now pouring in fast from burst pipes in adjoining tanks and rising up to our shoulders. Harrington tried to hold my hand but it slipped and he died in the oil.

There was another boy called Harrison clinging to a stanchion. I tried to lift him above the level of the oil but he screamed blue murder for he had broken both collar bones and an ankle. All this time I was swallowing oil. Gradually the oil found its level and stopped rising. Everything went very quiet.

The hatch above us was sealed and we had no idea if the ship was afloat, partly submerged or at the bottom of the ocean. We must have been there nearly an hour when the miracle happened. The hatch was prized open and three stokers came down with ropes and pulled us to safety.   Above, on the fo'c'sle deck outside the galley, Engine Room Artificer Robert Sherriff was standing talking to the Chief Cook, 'Dolly' Gray. The explosion split the deck open where they were standing and both fell through. Sherriff managed to cling to a projecting ledge and regain the deck but the Chief Cook was propelled on downward and was never seen again.

Supply Petty Officer Arthur Start, who with his mate Petty Officer Bob Walkey managed to save several trapped men, relates.

I was in the PO's mess at the time the first torpedo hit. All the lights went out but fortunately I happened to have a torch in my pocket. Chief Petty Officers and Petty Officers came running from everywhere and as I had the only torch I led them up to the flight deck where in such an event we had been told to muster. Realising that the messdecks below might still contain trapped men, we lifted back the hatch cover of the vertical shaft down through which the gold had been lowered. Sure enough within the compartment we could see men swimming around in oil and water. My mate ran to fetch ropes and ladders but while he was away several of the men below managed to get into the shaft which was only two feet square. Within the trunking there were no ridges or ledges to provide a hold but in desperation those men somehow managed to come up through by working their knees and backs against the sides. Eventually the hatch was sealed. There were several men down there but they were dead anyway.

By now many of the ship's company were assembled on the boat and flight decks awaiting orders. The general hubbub of conversation hushed as the figure of Captain Faulkner appeared hurrying down from the bridge. Few commanding officers can have been so popular with their men. Here was a captain in whom they unreservedly placed their trust. A leader they would follow anywhere. His features, normally cheerful, were now grim and stern. As he faced his men, many dripping in oil fuel, he paused only long enough to tell them that if all the correct procedures were carried out he had high hopes of getting the ship's company back to Murmansk. Morale could not have been higher and a great cheer went up from the crew. As Captain Faulkner later stated in his report to Admiralty, 'The way they responded convinced me that my hopes were shared by all and that the morale of the crew was indeed high'. But as his gaze fell on the twisted remains of the quarter deck, silhouetted like a mass of obscene sculpture, stark and tall against the cold light of the Arctic afternoon, he said abruptly, 'The admiral had accepted full responsibility'. The remark and the way it was expressed left the crew in no doubt there had been some degree of difference in decisions taken between him and the admiral from the time *Edinburgh* had left the convoy to the actual torpedoing. With that he saluted and hurried away.

As the day wore on, many acts of heroism and tragedy occurred in and around the explosion areas. Men trapped in small compartments pulled to safety in the nick of time as oil threatened to engulf them. Men caught in the blast of burst steam pipes in darkness until the flesh peeled from their bodies. Men trapped alive in unreachable compartments, a voice tube the only link with the upper deck, as officers tried

EDINBURGH IS TORPEDOED   69

to reassure them they would soon be freed knowing full well survival time was running out.

For Captain Faulkner, the safety of his men and the safety of the ship were his only concern. If the vessel could remain afloat with all watertight doors and hatches securely locked and if the surviving engine room could produce sufficient power to move the cruiser, no matter how slowly, the chances of reaching the Kola inlet were high. Following the torpedo explosions, he tried to establish contact with the lower steering position and the damage control post right aft but neither here nor in 'Y' cabin flat near where the torpedo had struck could he raise an answer. In the event he ordered the starboard tubes to be fired to reduce the list on that side.

In the meantime the convoy, several miles to the north, was still proceeding westward. A signal was passed to *Bulldog* reporting that *Edinburgh* had been torpedoed and requesting assistance. But Commander Maxwell Richmond had his hands full with his own problems. U boats had been sighted astern and ahead of the convoy and the escorts were speeding around depth-charging the enemy in an attempt to ward off an attack. Amidst this flurry of activity and loth to spare his escorts, he orderd Commander Salter of *Foresight* to take *Forester* and the two Russian destroyers with him to investigate.

It was 5.30 p.m. before they could reach the stricken cruiser, to find to their relief that enough steam pressure had been raised to turn one propeller slowly. The great ship was indeed in a sorry state. The explosion amidships had opened up her side for some 50 feet exposing ruptured compartments almost through to the port side. Hundreds of tons of sea water were swamping through the great hole, tearing at bulkheads fractured and buckled by the blast. Aft, 63 feet of tangled wreckage of the stern and the two pulverised shafts hung deep in the water, which pulled her down by the stern and acting as a rudder, made her totally unmanageable.

Below decks, men worked desperately, often with only a torch, to get all kinds of machinery operating or to set up hastily rigged alternative sources of power.

Attempts were now made to try to tow the cruiser back to the Kola Inlet 250 miles away. A formidable task indeed. With *Foresight* and the two Russian destroyers screening the cruiser from further U boat attacks, *Forester* managed to pass a tow to *Edinburgh*'s fo'c'sle. It was a grim experience. The piercing cold wind had turned the decks into a sheet of ice, making it difficult to maintain a footing. Seamen worked in unbearable conditions handling wires cumbersome and almost unmanageable because of icing. Eventually, a wire was secured and *Forester* taking up the slack began to tow. But by now *Edinburgh* was a dead weight. Each time the little destroyer took the strain on the wire it brought the cruiser up into the wind; an awkward tow, with the ship yawing clumsily from side to side. The admiral and Captain Faulkner watched anxiously as the tow whipped out of the water, hurling a shower of spray as it pulled momentarily taut and then plunged back into the sea, while *Forester* responded sluggishly to the sudden heave. Each time it lifted to bar tautness quivering under the strain it seemed as though it might be the last. As the wind-swept rollers met the massive weight of the hull, lifting the bow to run swiftly under the ship, the strident noise of creaking and jarring came from the tortured metal amidships and astern. Minutes later, the tow unequal to the excessive demands made upon it, snapped with a report like that of a rifle shot. The wire, like an uncoiled spring, lashed back to whip across the fo'c'sle deck to tangle itself around bollards and stanchions. Four attempts later, all unsuccessful, the undertaking to tow from the bow was abandoned.

The situation improved a little when with the aid of acetylene cutters some of the tangled wreckage at the stern dropped off but there was still a considerable section protruding below that acted as an unwanted rudder, turning her on a circular course to port. It was decided that *Forester* should pass a line aft to control the stern action, while *Edinburgh* tried to make some movement forward under her own steam. Before this could take place, however, a U boat was sighted on the surface barely three miles astern by an efficient young lookout. In all probability this was U boat 456. Teichert could not resist taking a good look at the destruction he had accomplished, at the same time reporting the position of the damaged cruiser to base. Determined to make a kill, *Forester*'s commanding officer, Lieut-Commander George Huddart, ordered full speed ahead. In the engine room, excitement was high as the engineers slammed levers to full throttle. With the ship vibrating and shaking enough to loosen every rivet, *Forester* at her top speed of 33 knots rapidly approached the position where the U boat was seen to dive. As they neared, speed was reduced to allow the asdic-dome to be lowered. From this they would be able to detect the enemy in the depths below. But Teichert's luck held, for on the bridge of *Forester* Huddart received from the engine room the bitterly frustrating report that the throttles, so energetically thrown open to maximum speed earlier, had jammed in that position and speed could not be reduced. It must have been a bitter blow to his hopes of levelling the score as the destroyer raced on over the submerged submarine unable to stop. It was sometime before the defect could be remedied and the ship return to the target area to begin the hunt. It was also found that the asdic-recorder had frozen solid and was incapable of receiving echo marks. A couple of random depth charges were dropped, the search abandoned and *Forester*, her decks covered with frozen spray and with the forward gun iced up, returned to *Edinburgh* unable to encourage the admiral with news of a kill. Unknown to Huddart, however, *Forester*'s mission had not been entirely without success. When the surfaced *U456* observed the destroyer heading rapidly in her direction, Teichert had ordered a crash dive which carried her deep and away from the course of the British ship. Having stopped engines he waited, silent, listening to the throb of the destroyer's screws above him. But later, when *Forester* returned and depth-charged the area, by a hundred-to-one chance one of the two charges damaged the periscope and rendered it inoperable. Unable to observe except by surfacing, a risk he was not prepared to take, Teichert could only lie submerged listening to the sounds of the British cruiser and its escorts. He was quite content to wait, knowing that in a few hours support would be arriving from Kirkenes.

By the time *Forester* returned, *Foresight* had succeeded in passing a wire tow from the fo'c'sle into *Edinburgh* right aft. The cruiser was now moving slowly forward towing *Foresight*, allowing the destroyer to act as a rudder to keep her on course. This proved reasonably successful and during that night and the early hours of Friday morning, 1 May, the little group moved steadily southward towards the Kola inlet at three knots. The bitter Polar wind brought with it more snow and a visibility varying from two to eight miles. Despite the critical situation, Captain Faulkner had reasonable hope that *Edinburgh* could reach Murmansk. But at 6 o'clock that morning the two escorting Russian destroyers signalled they were running short of fuel and would have to return to Murmansk to replenish. This was indeed a setback. With only two destroyers in attendance, the admiral decided that both would have to be used to maintain a screen against any U boat which might be clinging to their tail. It was an accurate assumption, for unknown to the admiral, *U456* was following the cruiser from a safe distance and, still submerged, listening to the bustling activities on the surface.

In the event *Foresight*'s tow was cast off. The two Russian destroyers disappeared in the poor visibility and the two British destroyers began their screening patrol around the cruiser. Almost at once *Edinburgh* again started her bizarre motions, at time going quite out of control by performing complete circles. Only by the superb seamanship of the captain were these antics checked and a forward course sustained, although her speed had dropped to two knots. Stokers and engine room staff performed a magnificent job. The engine room register showed that in one watch 64 separate orders were executed. However, a disturbing feature of their crawling course to Murmansk was the tortuous tack winding astern, indicated by a broad oil slick which disclosed their course as surely as any signpost.

As if *Edinburgh* had not enough troubles to cope with, a signal from the Senior British Naval Officer – Murmansk, Admiral Robert Hesketh Bevan, now reported, '... many enemy submarines are taking up positions between *Edinburgh* and the Kola inlet'. This was immediately followed by a signal from *Bulldog* indicating they had received a report from Admiralty that enemy destroyers were at sea heading for the convoy, or *Edinburgh*, or both.

However discouraging these reports, they were somewhat mitigated by a further signal from the SBNO – Murmansk reporting that a Russian tug was on its way in company with the British minesweepers *Harrier, Niger Hussar* and *Gossamer* which had only recently returned from their escort duty of QP11. With a pack of U boats lying in wait and a possible attack by enemy surface ships from the north or north-west, it was a race against time. True, the presence of the minesweepers would be some consolation but with their single 4-inch guns they could do little against the powerful modern 6-inch guns of the enemy. Even *Foresight* and *Forester* would be outgunned if the enemy were to attack.

In *Edinburgh*, the crew at action stations waited tense and restless, discussing the chances of reaching Murmansk before the enemy could find them. The temperature had dropped to 10 degrees below freezing. Destruction of one of the clothing stores had deprived a number of men of the warm clothing essential for those in exposed conditions. For these men it was sheer torture. The steady wind blowing off the Polar ice cap froze them to the marrow. With the main galley out of action it was sandwiches and cocoa for everyone. The only receptacles large enough in which to brew ship's cocoa were the officers' baths and these were immediately put into use. On look-out and open gun positions the men huddled together behind steel screens or deck lockers, trying to gain whatever warmth they could from one another. Men learned not to breathe too deeply because the shock of the cold air brought pain to the lungs. Like an insidious poison the deadly chill crept up from the feet and spread with unbelieving numbness. If a man was foolish enough to forget his gloves, a careless touch on exposed steel would peel off the flesh like paper. Eyebrows and eyelashes became white with frost. Even the tiny hairs in the nostrils became needle-sharp icicles, piercing the skin at a touch. With the contraction of metal, hatch covers jammed, door hinges and locks were frozen into immobility and gun breeches in exposed positions seized up and were useless.

On the bridge, grim faced and inwardly apprehensive, the admiral and Captain Faulkner, muffled and hooded, gazed out across the dark grey lifting sea with troubled eyes. On their shoulders rested the responsibility of saving the crippled ship, its crew and a fortune in gold bullion. Occasionally a large snow cloud reduced visibility to less than a mile to bring a mass of driving snow flakes, freezing as they fell on the already white, silent decks. And then with unpredictable suddenness the heavy cloud would be gone, leaving a visibility of eight miles or more. They had still 200 miles to cover and at the present speed of 2 knots it would be another four days and nights before they could reach the haven of Murmansk.

Late that night, *Edinburgh* received a further discouraging signal from Admiralty. It was that the pocket battleship

Admiral Scheer had left Trondheim, Norway and was loose in the Arctic. The *Scheer*, sister ship to the notorious *Graf Spee* which had been scuttled and sunk at Montevideo in 1939, was a formidable adversary. At the time it was considered that the only British ships which could meet them on equal terms were the capital ships *Renown* and *Repulse*. *Scheer*'s impressive armament amounted to six 11-inch guns, eight 6-inch and six 4-inch; these in addition to numerous anti-aircraft and lighter guns. Her fuel capacity and range of 19,000 miles at 19 knots allowed her to stay at sea for considerable periods.

It was in the midst of these disturbing signals that *Edinburgh* yawed her tortuous way southwards. If the *Scheer* should come upon her the end would be swift and certain. So far as Admiral Bonham-Carter and Captain Faulkner were concerned it was better not to think about it.

CHAPTER 5

The Destroyers' Brilliant Defence

MEANWHILE, TWO HUNDRED MILES to the north-west, the
QP11 convoy crept along the edge of the ice-barrier,
shepherded by the escorts led by *Bulldog*.

At 6 o'clock that morning, 1 May, the first German air
torpedo attack of the Arctic war took place.

As far as Arctic air strategy was concerned, far reaching
plans had been put into effect to employ this new form of air
strike against convoys. The long range aircraft each carrying
two torpedoes could launch their missiles at some distance
from target to bring confusion and disaster to any convoy.
Two distinguished Luftwaffe officers were responsible for
the structure and organisation of air operations in North
Norway. They were Major Blordon, operating the Junkers
88 Squadron KG30; and Colonel Ernst Roth, the flight
commander at Bardufoss conducting operations of the air
torpedo group, flying Heinkel 111s. German air bases had
benefited from reinforcements in an endeavour to destroy
every convoy moving eastward or westward. The strength
of the Luftwaffe in North Norway had reached a total of
103 JU88 long range bombers, 42 HE111 torpedo bombers,
15 HE115 torpedo bombers, 30 Stuka dive bombers and 74
long range reconnaisance aircraft (Blohm *und* Voss 138 and
FW Condors). The giant multi-engined Condors were vital
to the operation. They were able to fly long sweeps into the
Arctic to find convoys, shadow them and guide massed
bomber squadrons to the attack.

Low on the horizon a group of Heinkel 111s, appearing

as little dots at first, swept in from the south, their shape and size becoming more clearly defined as they approached. Barely 20 feet above the water, they came in line ahead in a wide circle, each carrying two torpedoes. If this new form of attack was intended to cower Richmond's forces into retreat, it was a gross miscalculation. On the flank of the convoy and closest to the attackers was the little corvette *Snowflake*. With her single 4-inch gun and two machine guns firing at maximum speed and efficiency, she raced towards the line of aircraft. The near shell blasts and accuracy of machine gun fire was so disconcerting that the bombers were unable to concentrate on their target and in an instant of confusion loosed their torpedoes, which sped on ineffectually to run harmlessly among the ice floes. During the next thirty minutes the bombers made repeated attempts to break through but without success. With their torpedoes expended and thwarted in their endeavours, the Heinkels returned to base.

At the German Naval Headquarters North Norway, Admiral Schmundt formulated the final details of his plan of attack. He must have been highly pleased with the turn of events. Fortune had bestowed on him a gift beyond his wildest hopes. Without any loss or harm to his own forces the supreme prize, the cruiser *Edinburgh*, had been eliminated as a fighting unit. Crippled and disabled, she was incapable of adopting her role as protective cover. The convoy to the north-west was now left virtually defenceless against the superior destroyer flotilla; a convoy which had counted on the presence of the cruiser to protect it from this very form of attack.

At 3 o'clock on the morning of 1 May 1942, a motor patrol boat carried a mission order to the command destroyer *Hermann Schoemann* at Kirkenes. Its purpose, 'Final destruction of the British cruiser and the annihilation of the convoy and escorts'. On paper the elimination of QP11 seemed a straightforward operation. The German ships with their overwhelming superior armament would first destroy the weak escort protection, then sink the merchant vessels one by one, and finally return to dispatch the helpless *Edinburgh*. Frustrated by constant inaction and the restraint on their attacking capabilities dictated by fuel limitations, the three heavy destroyers were off at once. Their first objective, the convoy.

Teichert's report from *U456* made it clear that the crippled cruiser could be attacked at any time at the speed she was maintaining, whereas the convoy moving slowly but steadily west might soon be outside their range of operations. At one o'clock that day in 73 degrees north, 25 degrees east the German destroyers came upon the convoy and its escorts in poor visibility and constant snow showers and prepared to attack.

The senior escort officer Commander Richmond was already burdened with enough problems without this impending threat. Apart from the Heinkel attack which had been beaten off but would possibly be renewed, numbers of U boats were sighted astern obviously waiting for the opportunity to close in. Wisely he avoided the temptation to dispatch his escorts to chase the submarines and thereby reduce the defence of the convoy. Instead he closed the screen around the merchant ships daring the enemy to break through. Almost at the same time heavy pack ice was sighted to the north and west. Immense masses of drifting ice extending 15 miles southward lay across their path. Richmond had no alternative but to order the convoy to steer south-west. His hopes of shaking off the U boats were dashed. To reduce the number of directions from which an attack could be launched he shepherded the merchant ships in among the ice floes. At least the starboard flank was protected. Now in this anxious state of affairs came the report which he dreaded most.

At 1.45 that afternoon *Snowflake* on the port beam

reported three unidentified radar contacts to the south, and then from the destroyer *Beverley*, slightly ahead, came the signal, 'Enemy in sight – Three destroyers'. Almost at once the flash of gunfire was seen from the approaching ships and shells began falling among the convoy. In a desperate attempt to avoid the shellfire the master of the SS *Briarwood*, Commodore William Lawrence, led his ships towards the ice edge and broke through a wide barrier to steam circumspectly up through channels between ice packs. It was a bold but risky venture, for if the screws sustained damage a ship could be trapped, helpless. Against this, the chances of torpedoes reaching their targets between the ice masses were minimised. After signalling *Edinburgh* that the convoy was being attacked by enemy destroyers, *Bulldog* steamed across the front of the convoy at full speed, calling for *Amazon, Beverley* and *Beagle* to join her. On the bridge beneath Richmond's feet the destroyer's decks trembled as she increased her speed and the wind struck ice-cold on his face. At the guns, loaded and ready, crews stood waiting while the ship sped over the black water and the range shortened. In line ahead, with the destroyers between the convoy and the enemy, the British ships opened fire. It was a naval engagement worthy of the finest traditions of the Royal Navy, for academically the British ships should have been utterly destroyed. On the one side Richmond's forces carried 4.7-inch guns, whereas the German ships mounted 5.9-inch guns.

Despite the overwhelming superiority of the attackers, their assault was somewhat constrained by orders from German High Command that their precious ships must not be subjected to risk. Against this was the determination of the British that the convoy would be defended to the bitter end. Repeatedly the two destroyer forces, in line ahead and on parallel courses, blazed away at one another with both sides loosing torpedoes. Each time the enemy turned to double back on their last course, *Bulldog* and her consorts turned also, always keeping themselves between the enemy and the convoy. Frequently the British ships were bracketed with heavy shells as the enemy tried to establish the range, but with each salvo falling to port or starboard the British force manoeuvered into a new line of advance.

Of a sudden, *Amazon*, second in line, was caught in a salvo that straddled her in a sudden sheet of flame and black smoke. Still in line and maintaining top speed, she sped on. As the smoke cleared, her captain Lieutenant-Commander Lord Teynham, stunned and bruised from the explosion, looked down from the bridge on a scene of destruction. The forward gun had been torn from its mounting; its crew dead or wounded lay prone on the fo'c'sle deck. The 4.7-inch gun aft, the 4-inch amidships and the anti-aircraft guns had been smashed with their crews killed or wounded. The wheelhouse was shattered and the main and auxiliary steering positions rendered untenable.

Careering along at 30 knots she was now out of control. As *Bulldog* made a tight turn to double back on the previous course, *Amazon* could only speed onward. And it was only by cleverly executed manoeuvres of the engines that her captain was able to bring her back into line at the rear of the column. She was immobilized as a fighting unit but it would not do to let the enemy be aware of this. Despite the fearful damage the ship had sustained, Lord Teynham somehow managed to maintain *Amazon* in line, so that to the enemy she still appeared a potential threat. Unable to break through and with shells from the British ships falling around them, the enemy at last turned away.

To give some protection to the convoy, Richmond, with thick black smoke pouring from the funnels of his ship, laid a smoke screen between them and the convoy.

At 2.30 p.m. the German destroyers returned, approaching from the south-east. Without hesitation, *Bulldog* came around in a tight circle at speed, heading directly for them, a fountain of waves creaming back from her slim bows. There was an aggressive appearance about the ship as she sped on with clouds of spray breaking over the forward deck. The lean grey destroyer, slicing into the deep troughs, rising high on the shoulder of the next wave, made it manifestly clear she was committed to the destruction of the enemy.

The sight of the formidable little ship racing towards them, her guns blazing, must have given rise to some misgivings, for after recklessly firing more torpedoes the enemy rapidly turned away. In some respects it was not unlike the resolute naval action in 1591, when Sir Richard Grenville in his small flagship *Revenge* tore into the fleet of fifty-three Spanish galleons destroying four of the great ships before his own vessel was rendered useless.

Meanwhile the convoy was in trouble. The German torpedoes running loose among the ice floes from the last encounter rose to the surface in a trail of bubbles to speed on towards the merchant ships. A straggler, the Russian freighter *Ciolkovsky* was dead in line. The sudden explosion as the torpedo plunged into the engine room rocked her to a standstill. Almost casually she settled down by the bows, her screws high out of water, poised for the plunge. With the pungent smell of oil from her ruptured tanks came cries for help as the crew tried to launch rafts and boats.

The port lifeboat, although overcrowded was successfully floated off but on the starboard side panic prevailed. Twenty-five of the crew had managed to climb into the boat with the davits swung out, poised over the water some thirty feet below ready for lowering. Unfortunately the stern fall had jammed in the reel, slightly tilting it. Despite all efforts to release the obstruction matters worsened with the weight of those in the boat. In the confusion that followed one of the two men operating the lowering mechanism took an axe in a moment of panic and severed the fall. The boat swung down hanging by the bow, throwing every man into the sea. In increasing terror, the second fall was now cut and the heavy boat plummeted down on to the men below, killing many of those swimming around. Moments later the ship plunged slowly to her grave, with a small crowd of men packed high in the stern waving and screaming for help.

In minutes, the trawler *Lord Middleton* was among them. Those who had survived the explosion and the numbing shock of immersion were hauled aboard more dead than alive. Saturated in the black oil, it was difficult to grasp the men and lift them over the side. After thirty minutes of search only a pathetic collection of bodies remained, washing about among the oil and mass of wreckage, and *Lord Middleton* made off at speed to join the distant convoy.

When *Bulldog* and her consorts rejoined the merchant ships she found them still among the ice, steaming up whatever lanes of open water they could find. Anxiously Richmond watched the distant horizon, convinced more attacks were to follow. A conviction that was well-founded.

Within an hour the enemy returned approaching this time from astern. Once more battle was joined. Encouraged by their earlier success the British destroyers rushed headlong towards the enemy but now the German ships had found the range and *Bulldog* was subjected to a hail of shell splashes, almost miraculously escaping a direct hit. Thwarted in this further attempt the German ships turned away. Richmond's courageous defence had so far prevented the enemy from breaking through. Had they done so the outcome would have been disastrous for the convoy, in single line, was now stretched out over a distance of seven miles.

Thirty minutes later from out of the low cloud the enemy returned again and once more strove to break through to the creeping convoy. Again and again they attacked, six times in all, and yet six times their hopes of destroying the convoy were denied. By now it was clear to Schulze-Hinrichs that Richmond and his forces were prepared to fight to the death rather than allow a break through in the defence line. It could be argued that the lengthy engagement by the German destroyers would have opened the way for a simultaneous attack by their U boats but it later emerged that lack of direct communication had made such co-operation between the two forces impossible.

By 6 o'clock that evening the German destroyers had used up nearly two-thirds of their ammunition. It must have been with a mixture of frustration, humiliation and bitter disappointment that Schulze-Hinrichs and his destroyer crews received orders from Admiral Schmundt to abandon the engagement and proceed to the south-east to find and destroy the crippled *Edinburgh*, 200 miles away. A far easier target they imagined than the convoy. As the German ships disappeared over the horizon, Richmond must have uttered a sigh of relief. The bluff had succeeded. Almost at once he signalled *Edinburgh* to report that the German forces had broken off the engagement and were heading in the direction of the cruiser. Battered and exhausted but stimulated by the success of their stubborn defence, *Bulldog* and her consorts rounded up the convoy and headed to the west and home.

Later that day, *Beverley*'s commanding officer Lieutenant Price signalled Commander Richmond, 'I should hate to play poker with you'.

CHAPTER 6

Crippled *Edinburgh* Fights On

IN THE MEANTIME, *Edinburgh* had made little progress
eastward. She was still maintaining a speed of 2 knots but
only by skilful deployment of her engines was she prevented
from going around in circles. It was a weary exercise but at
least they were moving and not lying immobile to present a
'sitting duck' target to watching U boats, whose presence
triggered off constant alarms to men continually closed up at
action stations. They may have kept the crews on their toes
but, exhausted, the men were running into debt to sleep,
eroding that knife-edged vigilance on which hope of
survival depended.

When Admiral Bonham-Carter received *Bulldog*'s signal of
the attack on the convoy he did so with considerable
disquietude. It was clear it would be only a matter of time
before the German flotilla would turn their attention to
Edinburgh and set about their destructive task. With only the
two small destroyers *Foresight* and *Forester* for protection, he
realised *Edinburgh* would be in an almost indefensible
situation. Even if they arrived in time, the small group of
minesweepers racing up from the south could give little
support. He therefore dispatched the following signal to his
two destroyers to be repeated to the minesweepers, who
signalled their present position and gave estimated time of
arrival around midnight.

In the event of attack by German destroyers, *Foresight*
and *Forester* are to act independently taking every

opportunity to defeat the enemy without taking undue risks to themselves in defending *Edinburgh*.

Edinburgh is to proceed wherever the wind permits, probably straight into it. If the minesweepers are present they are also to be told to act independently, retiring under smoke screens as necessary. *Edinburgh* has no direction finder or director working.

The signal came as a welcome relief to Lieut-Commander George Huddart of *Forester* and to Commander Jocelyn Salter of *Foresight*, for discharged from the responsibility of having to act in a purely defensive role they could now adopt whatever measures were necessary to meet the changing situation.

All through the afternoon of 1 May 1942, red-eyed and weary look-outs searched the distant horizon. At 6 o'clock a small ship was spotted coming up from the south-east. As it neared it proved to be a Russian tug, the *Rubin*, her mission to tow the cruiser to Murmansk, and preparations were put in hand to perform the difficult task of securing a wire to *Edinburgh*'s bows. Just before midnight with the sun touching the horizon and immediately rising again, the four British minesweepers hove in sight. They were *Hussar*, *Harrier*, *Gossamer* and *Niger*, each armed with two 4-inch guns.

Hopes were raised as the little flotilla of ships gathered around the cruiser but they were soon dashed when it turned out that the tug was not powerful enough to tow the big ship on her own. After a number of attempts two tows were eventually secured. One from *Edinburgh*'s starboard bow to the tug and another from *Gossamer* to the port quarter. While this manoeuvre assisted in keeping her on course the speed of 2 knots was barely improved.

By 5.30 on the morning of 2 May this disposition was completed, with a screen of *Foresight* and *Forester* on either beam and *Harrier*, *Niger* and *Hussar* stationed astern.

After failing in their attempt to destroy the convoy the German destroyers steamed speedily to the south-east. It would be an easy matter to find the British cruiser for Teichert was still following the ship from a safe distance. All through that night the flotilla raced on at 35 knots. This second set-back in three weeks left Schulze-Hinrichs grimly determined that the order from Admiral Schmundt, 'destruction of the cruiser *Edinburgh*', would be executed.

His plan was to approach the cruiser from the north with the wind behind him and his destroyers in line abreast, a little over a mile apart. Immediately they were in effective firing range they were to turn together and fire all torpedoes at the same time. On this wide front of attack he considered it improbable that *Edinburgh*, now incapable of manoeuvring, could escape from such a concentration of cross-fire. Following the attack his destroyers were to take cover within the nearest fog bank.

Just after 6 o'clock that morning a long black oil slick was spotted trailing southward. All the indications were that *Edinburgh* could not now be far away. Intermittent snow showers varied the visibility from two to eight miles. Fifteen minutes later one of the German ships *Z25* reported a silhouette to starboard and the three destroyers immediately altered course. It was the quarry they were seeking – HMS *Edinburgh*.

Hardly had the British minesweepers taken up their screening positions when *Hussar* saw the German destroyers looming out of the mist. Immediately the little ship opened fire with her two 4-inch guns. Thus began the opening of a new phase in the operations. As boldly as *Bulldog* had defied attack from the heavily armed destroyers, *Hussar* now took up the challenge with a spirited and gallant resistance to the enemy. But finally, outgunned and outmanoeuvered and straddled by shells, she had no recourse but to fall back and seek support from the two British destroyers. As the first gun flashes showed through the mist, *Edinburgh* cast off the tow lines and increased speed to her maximum of 8 knots. Despite the inevitable circling to port the measure seemed preferable to remaining stopped. By now the Germans were finding the range and several falls of shot were registered astern of the cruiser. At once *Foresight*'s and *Forester*'s telegraphs rang 'full speed ahead', and with waves creaming back from the bows they turned in a flurry of foam towards the enemy, guns blazing defiantly.

If the earlier engagement between the German flotilla and Richmond's forces had been one-sided in terms of fire power, this action was even more so. The enemy's combined armament of twelve 5.9-inch guns were now ranged against eight 4.7-inch guns and some of these were frozen and could not be used. *Foresight* speeding towards the enemy at 31 knots and *Forester* a cable length astern now turned together and fired a spread of torpedoes. And *Edinburgh*, slowly and painfully yawing round into the wind, was to prove she was still a power to be reckoned with. With her battle flag streaming in the wind and her heavy 6-inch shells waiting in the guns of her one and only operational turret, the cruiser opened fire. A moment later, as the German destroyers *Z24*, *Z25* and the *Hermann Schoemann* crossed the line of fire, *Edinburgh*'s guns again flashed out. Now followed a wild, intermittent fight as the German and British ships raced in and out of the snow squalls and smoke screens laid by both sides. It was then that the admiral received the welcome message from Admiralty that the German battleship *Scheer* was now back in Trondheim harbour. With all the depressing news and set-backs of the last few days the signal came as a relief despite the critical situation in which they now found themselves.

As *Edinburgh* completed another circle, bringing her bows around to face the enemy, the guns of 'B' turret were ready and waiting. With the director out of action and no power to move the turret itself, firing and spotting orders were given by the young turret officer Lieutenant R. M. Howe, who had his head and shoulders out through the hatch at the top. At that moment, the leading enemy destroyer *Hermann Schoemann* came into view running out of the shelter of a snow cloud. Howe gave the order 'Fire', and the cruiser's guns roared out in an ear-splitting crash, the muzzles spewing long tongues of flame and black smoke. Considering the encumbering circumstances, the firing was remarkably accurate. The first salvo fell within a few yards of the German destroyer and in desperation she tried to turn away towards her own smoke screen, heeling over at an alarming angle. It was a forlorn attempt. Even as her guns replied, those of *Edinburgh* thundered out in a mass of flame. This time the shells found her in an ear-splitting holocaust of fire and smoke. The tremendous explosion lifted the deck structure, smashing it through the hull like cardboard. Above and below decks men were hurled into one another and against steel bulkheads in a sickening crash. Both engine rooms were destroyed and with all control systems out of action the *Hermann Schoemann* drifted to a stop.

This action altered the outlook completely. For his remarkable feat of gunnery Lieutenant R. M. Howe was later awarded the DSC. The opening phase of the engagement had not been marked by any gallant endeavour on the part of the German ships to smash their way through the flimsy protective screen of escorts and this setback changed their original offensive posture into one of defence. Their purpose now seemed to be to rescue the crew of the command ship while still putting down a heavy barrage of fire. Even their rescue endeavour was frustrated by the tenacity of the two British destroyers in their probing thrusts.

At the time *Schoemann* was hit *Foresight* and *Forester* were steaming at speed, independently seeking the enemy ships among the scurrying snow clouds. From one of these flurries Commander Salter of *Foresight* saw one of the

German ships emerge heading straight for him. Swinging his ship to starboard to deliver a salvo from his four guns a sudden gust of smoke and cloud obscured the target but on his port beam, Lieut-Commander Huddart of *Forester* found he was ideally placed to fire torpedoes at the advancing German and immediately turned to starboard. As *Forester* turned, the full fury of the enemy's vastly superior armament fell on the ship. One shell, plunging through the hull, severely damaged the forward and after boiler rooms, killing and injuring many stokers and ERAs, and bringing the ship to a stop in an eruption of cloud and steam. Another shell, striking aft, killed the captain of the gun and injured two others, and a third passed through the gun shield of the forward gun near the bridge to explode in a sheet of flame. It was a splinter from this shell which killed Lieut-Commander Huddart who was leaning over the bridge superstructure exhorting 'B' gun's crew to greater efforts. Three of 'B' gun's crew were also killed from the explosion. The breechworker was severely hit in the head and was believed dead. Miraculously he recovered consciousness and during a lull in the fighting started walking to the sick bay, but he passed out on the fo'c'sle where he was found and taken aft. He was to die in hospital several days later.

Within five minutes two more shells struck the ship. One in the issue room killing three men outright and injuring eight others and another in the RDF office killing the two operators. On the death of his commanding officer, Lieutenant Jack Bitmead, RN took over command and continued the action.

Forester now lay stopped less than two miles from the guns of the enemy ships but seeing her sister ship in this perilous situation *Foresight*, with black smoke pouring from her funnels, gallantly placed herself between *Forester* and the enemy and in doing so drew upon herself a concentration of accurate fire. Immediately she received two direct hits, one like *Forester* in the forward boiler room and the other aft. Again there were many casualties. It left her with only one gun in action. Among the killed were the first lieutenant, Lieut-Commander Richard Fawdrey, RN, and a passenger, Captain Stone, master of the freighter *Lancaster Castle*. Fortunately one boiler room was still operational and although badly damaged she was able to retire very slowly towards *Edinburgh* which was still engaged in her circular antics and firing whenever her bows faced the enemy. *Forester*, helpless and stopped almost under the guns of the enemy destroyers, awaited the final blow.

So close were they, there was now the alternative possibility of being boarded and the ship captured and Lieutenant Bitmead ordered one of the young midshipmen to throw the confidential books overboard. These contained the secret codes used throughout the Home Fleet operating in northern waters to decipher signals. To prevent the enemy capturing them and thereby gaining access to secret information passing between Admiralty and ships, the standard procedure was to ditch the books over the side, firmly secured in heavily weighted bags. In the excitement and turmoil of battle the young midshipman could not find a sufficient number of weighted bags and carried out the order by throwing all the confidential papers and pads over the side. While many sank a quantity stayed floating on the surface. Not immediately recognising the nature of the papers spread over the water around the ship, Bitmead asked, 'What are those tombola tickets doing floating off the starboard side?' The disclosure of what had happened resulted in the biggest scramble in the Home Fleet for some time for it threatened the very core of our secret communications. An Admiralty Board of Enquiry was quickly set up but from its findings the midshipman was happily exonerated.

While below decks stokers and engineers prayed, sweated and worked among the wreckage to restart the engines, officers and lookout crews on the bridge watched in horror as two torpedo tracks were seen racing towards them. Frozen into a state of immobility they waited for the shattering explosion which might well kill them all but in that unforgettable moment of terror the two killer torpedoes passed under, missing the keel by a hair's breadth and sped under and onward in the direction of *Edinburgh*. Conscious of their incredible escape, *Forester*'s crew redoubled their efforts to repair the fractured steam pipes and the most serious damage and to get under way again, well aware that at any moment another torpedo or another shell could find them. Meanwhile the torpedoes which had passed beneath *Forester* were nearing the end of their run, with one on course beginning to splash along the surface losing speed. *Edinburgh*, slowly completing another circuit, was now bearing round to cross its path on a collision course. In seconds, the torpedo struck the ship dead centre and for the third time the cruiser lifted and shuddered under the impact of the explosion. Engaged as they were in the violent gun battle the enemy ships were quite unaware of this. It was a bonus they hardly deserved. For *Edinburgh* this was the final blow. It was clear there was no hope of saving her. Yet her guns continued firing, the shells falling close around the German ships. The captain of one of the two active German destroyers remarked laconically, 'Her shooting is remarkably good'. Altogether a total of fifteen torpedoes were fired by the enemy in this one encounter.

For the moment let us leave *Edinburgh* and return to the plight of the two British destroyers, for it was on them that the fury of the enemy's guns was now being directed. In *Forester*'s engine and boiler rooms the extraordinary efforts of the crew had brought a measure of success and they reported they could raise enough steam to get the ship moving again. At once *Forester* turned away retiring slowly towards *Foresight* and *Edinburgh*. She was repeatedly straddled by shells but by executing a violent zig-zag course managed to deny the enemy another direct hit. As she returned still firing from astern, her after gun well into its 80th round, she scored a hit on the German destroyer *Z25*, producing a brilliant flash. But the other active destroyer *Z24* was now finding the range of *Foresight*, which could barely defend herself. Increasing her speed slowly to 12 knots, *Forester* closed in on her sister ship and by producing black funnel smoke shielded her from the enemy, again drawing on herself *Z24*'s fire. Lieutenant Bitmead was repaying his debt to Commander Salter. At the same time the gallant little minesweepers were playing their part in defence of the cruiser. Time and time again they darted forward firing their guns and behaving, as the Admiralty said later, 'like young terriers'.

Almost unbelievably, the minesweepers' valiant action in the cloud and flame of battle led the enemy to suppose they were destroyers arriving to supplement the British force and probably restrained them from mounting further attacks. In reality there was nothing but the small group of minesweepers to stop the Germans from annihilating every British ship opposing them. With the *Schoemann* completely disabled and *Z25* slightly damaged, the Germans broke off the engagement, eventually getting alongside the command ship to rescue the survivors. Setting charges, they scuttled the ship and made off for Kirkenes, damaged, dismayed and sadly disillusioned.

The German account of the engagement provided some highly interesting and dramatic details. It had been 6.15 that morning when the three German destroyers had spotted *Edinburgh* through the snow clouds and immediately opened fire. The range between the opposing forces was much closer than planned. Nearest to the enemy was the command destroyer *Hermann Schoemann* and she raced straight ahead amidst a hail of shell-fire from the British ships. On board there were frantic efforts to change the torpedo settings from 'long range', as earlier ordered, to 'short'. Seven minutes later Schulze-Hinrichs ordered all ships to turn and fire but at that moment a sudden snow squall obstructed *Z24* and *Z25*'s view of the cruiser and they held their fire. The *Schoemann* was 800 yards ahead when the order was given and as she turned to provide accurate launching of torpedoes three large water spouts were registered 100 yards astern indicating 6-inch shell bursts. They were now aware that some of the fire was coming from the crippled *Edinburgh*. For a disabled ship, at the mercy of the German flotilla, the gunfire was alarmingly accurate. Moments later a salvo struck the ship with devastating effect. Both engine rooms were destroyed, electricity supplies cut, control systems and armament put out of action, all at one stroke. In the words of *Schoemann*'s captain Heinrich Wittig, 'That the cruiser should have managed to hit such vital areas of the ship was the worst possible luck that could have overtaken us'.

Schoemann's turn to starboard slowly diminished as she lost way and took on the role of a sitting duck. Although smoke floats were thrown overboard several British destroyers avoided the smoke screen and again opened fire, while *Schoemann* attempted to defend herself with single shots. With fire control destroyed, one gun was fired over open sights by Petty Officer Diekmann and fired manually by Lieutenant Lietz, while entirely on their own initiative Petty Officers Keufgens and Schumacher operated two guns aft. Although one torpedo had been launched before *Schoemann* was hit the firing mechanism of the other tubes was jammed and the torpedo officer went to the forward position hoping to be able to fire individual torpedoes. The after tubes were impacted in one position but in spite of this three torpedoes were discharged as an enemy destroyer crossed the line of fire. With a muffled roar in the explosion chambers the deadly tin fish shot from the long sleek tubes, hung in the air and then with a simultaneous splash plunged beneath the surface to speed swiftly on their way towards the British ship.

Schoemann's chief engineer officer, Lieutenant Lorenz Bohmer, had checked the destruction below and confirmed that both engines were useless. Despite efforts to control the fires and escapes of steam the areas below decks became untenable. The ship had now become a stationary target for the British forces. It was clear that the *Hermann Schoemann* was doomed, and Wittig issued the final order, 'Prepare to blow up the ship – destroy secret documents and take life-saving equipment'. When she had been hit electric power to serve the radio transmitter had failed but one of the operators had succeeded in getting a short wave set going so that the flotilla commander Schulze-Hinrichs could contact the other ships.

By now *Z24* and *Z25* had laid down a smoke screen to cover the *Schoemann* and had renewed their bombardment of the enemy. Sighting the cruiser and a destroyer, the commanding officer of *Z25*, Lieut-Commander Peters, fired a salvo of four torpedoes. One of these struck *Edinburgh* her fatal blow but none of the German officers and crew were aware of this, engaged as they were in the gun battle with the British destroyers.

Immobilizing *Forester* by accurate fire from her 5.9-inch guns and severely damaging *Foresight*, *Z25* darted back to provide a further smoke screen for *Hermann Schoemann*. The screen also provided invaluable aid to her sister ship *Z24* which in spite of the gunfire she was being subjected to was trying to come alongside the *Schoemann* to rescue the crew. The several attempts proved extremely difficult and dangerous and finally ended in failure. About 7.30 a.m., Schulze-Hinrichs transmitted the message, 'Calling all ships. Am abandoning ship. *Schoemann* is finished'. Immediately *Z24* replied, 'Can we still come alongside?', to which came the reply, 'Yes, but hurry'. A few minutes later *Z25*, half a mile distant, received a direct hit in the signals office causing many casualties.

It was not until 8.00 a.m. that *Z24*, her guns still firing, managed to come to within a few feet of *Schoemann* enabling a few men to jump across. Fifteen minutes later, with shells falling all around, a final, successful attempt was made and the two destroyers secured alongside. Very quickly the whole crew, except for the killed and those who had escaped in boats and rafts, were taken off. Even the wounded, operated on by the surgeon-commander as the battle progressed were passed across, naked except for their bandages.

Aboard the doomed vessel, while boiler room floor valves were opened a petty officer on the quarterdeck laid a depth charge and set the time fuse. Finally, First Lieutenant Konrad Loerke, the only man left on the ship, clambered down into the fire computing section and pulled the fuse of a second depth charge. Then hastily pushing off from the destroyer in a life raft he was picked up by one of the boats. Minutes later the two depth charges exploded in a mighty roar and the *Hermann Schoemann* lifting her bows high in the air sunk quickly into the ice-floed waters of the Barents Sea with the cheers of the men on the rafts and in the boats ringing weirdly across the cold dark waters.

Meanwhile *Z24* and *Z25*, incapable of renewing the engagement, especially *Z24* with 250 of the *Schoemann*'s crew aboard, began their withdrawal. The flotilla commander realising there was no time or opportunity to stop and pick up the survivors in the boats and rafts now broke the rules of W/T silence by transmitting the message on U boat wavelengths, 'Square 5917. Save *Schoemann* survivors'. Aboard *U88*, Lieutenant Heino Bohmann heard the call for help and after being given the exact bearing by the destroyers set off for the position. Six hours later the U boat surfaced and picked up another 56 men. Already half dead from cold and exposure they were taken into the comparative warmth of the submarine to thaw out. From this rescue only one man died.

Total casualties aboard the two German destroyers amounted to 18 dead and 38 wounded. For the Germans with their total flotilla strength of three precious destroyers it had been a costly encounter. With one sunk and another badly damaged needing extensive repairs, it would be some months before they could mount another operation.

CHAPTER 7

The Destruction of *Z26*

THE BATTLE OF THE ARCTIC had arrived in all its fury. Prior to the loss of the *Schoemann*, on 2 May the Germans had lost another destroyer, *Z26*. Commanded by George Ritter von Berger she had been sunk in an engagement with the British cruiser *Trinidad*, when her consorts *Z24* and *Z25* had been able to rescue only 76 out of a crew of 320.

In this engagement, the brand new 'Colony' class cruiser HMS *Trinidad* of 8000 tons was escorting the convoy PQ13 to Murmansk. South of Bear Island on 29 March 1942, three German destroyers *Z24*, *Z25* and *Z26* had come upon the British forces in drifting clouds of thick fog and snow. Neither side could see the other to confirm recognition until the range had closed to only a little over a mile. Abruptly the fog cleared and in a flash *Trinidad* recognised the German ensign. Suddenly all hell broke loose. Each side with 6-inch calibre guns capable of firing fifteen miles were looking down one another's gun barrels. The range was so suicidally close that everything that could fire went into action – even machine guns. With devastating accuracy *Trinidad*'s salvoes crashed into and on the German ship, whose commanding officer Captain Ritter von Berger broke off the engagement and headed away into the cover of thick snow clouds after firing his port torpedoes. Anticipating the move, *Trinidad*'s commanding officer, Captain Leslie Saunders swung the cruiser violently to starboard in time to see the torpedo tracks pass dangerously close. Completing the turn he headed north in pursuit of the enemy. Despite decreasing visibility he was soon able to contact *Z26* by radar. With speed now at 30 knots the cruiser was quickly overhauling the German destroyer and soon the damaged ship was spotted with smoke and flame billowing from her decks and superstructure. At once *Trinidad* opened fire with her forward turrets and wiped out the enemy's after gun turrets. By now the German was taking terrible punishment and unable to reply could only zig-zag her course to avoid annihilation. In order to finish the German ship, *Trinidad* fired three torpedoes. Two of them were frozen in their mountings and failed to leave the tubes but the third sped on its way towards the destroyer.

But now something happened which made it the most singular and bizarre incident in British naval history. As the torpedo neared the German ship it started to veer off course and kept doing so until it had completed a half-circle and began heading back to the ship that fired it, *Trinidad*. Inconceivably, the gyro-mechanism controlling the torpedo rudder had jammed from the effects of the icing. It had run amok and with the whole of the Arctic Ocean in which to run wild it headed straight for the cruiser. Captain, officers and lookouts watched helplessly as the torpedo sped in to strike the ship dead amidships. The explosion was enormous, tearing away 60 feet of the ship's side. The disaster was unique and the probability of it happening about one in a million. It was in fact the only time in British naval history that a ship had torpedoed itself in battle.

The damage was disastrous causing many casualties. The worst area was in the transmitting room in the bottom of the ship. The explosion had ruptured the oil tanks above and all the men except four were drowned in the fuel which poured into the compartment. Although listing badly watertight doors kept the cruiser afloat and she was able to limp on at 5 knots towards the Kola inlet, eventually docking at Rosta where the Russians welded plates on to her torn side. In the meantime one of *Trinidad*'s accompanying destroyers *Eclipse* had caught up with *Z26*. There followed a crazy chase through the fog banks with *Eclipse*'s shells from her 4-inch gun slamming into the vessel which soon became stationary. But as *Eclipse* was about to fire her remaining torpedo the two German consorts *Z24* and *Z25* loomed out of the fog and began shelling her. With discretion the better part of valour she made off into the cover of low cloud to fight another day.

Out of the German destroyer's complement of 320 men, 246 were killed in the engagement. Among the survivors was the commanding officer Captain George Ritter von Berger, who was killed towards the end of the war. Many years later his widow wrote to the author giving her husband's account of the engagement.

As *Z26* was sinking, the Captain, although badly wounded in the face and legs managed to drag himself off the bridge and arriving at the rail gave the order to abandon ship. The men gave three cheers and jumped over the side into the icy water. As he floated away from the ship he was sure he would never be picked up alive but a life-boat from *Z24* arrived almost at once and he was carried aboard unconscious. Months later, having recovered from his wounds, he was appointed leader of the destroyer flotilla at Narvik in *Z32*.

When the Allied invasion of Normandy took place his ship was sunk in the English Channel and captured by the French he was imprisoned in the fortress of Gironde Sud. She then quotes.

In the night, my husband – being a prisoner alone in a house guarded by ragged soldiers – was brought to a lonely place and killed by machine guns. He was found some days later and buried in a cemetery at Berbuil Charente Maritime, near Saintes.

The outcome of the *Trinidad* and *Edinburgh* naval engagements was the temporary exclusion of the threat of attack on convoys by German destroyers based in North Norway since it was considered that those not sunk had been sufficiently damaged to be in need of repair. Against this however, the Germans stepped up their attacks by U boats and aircraft and by the end of the year 63 vessels had been sunk. It was by far the worst period throughout the whole of the Arctic war.

CHAPTER 8

The Last Hours

WE MUST NOW RETURN to HMS *Edinburgh* and to 0730 on 2 May when the loose torpedo was seen heading into the path of the cruiser. From the bridge Captain Faulkner watched in dismay as the torpedo approached, porpoising at the end of its run, the steel surface glistening evilly in the cold Arctic light. There was nothing he or anyone could do as cruiser and torpedo converged on an inevitable collision course.

On the bridge a very young signalman burst into tears in a mixture of fear and frustration. Someone turned and said, 'What's the matter, boy? Do you expect to live for ever?' As each man watched knowing this would be the end of their ship, Captain Faulkner turned to his fellow officers with, 'I think we're going to wear it this time – better grab a support and hold on'. The torpedo struck amidships on the port side almost opposite the area where the second torpedo had struck three days earlier. This latest assault cut her practically in two. There was one great shattering explosion accompanied by the noise of ripping tearing metal as the ship lurched to starboard and men began to die. With it came the unmistakable sound of tons of sea water flooding in under enormous pressure and the opposing elements of heat and cold as the hot blast from the explosion with its choking acrid fumes mingled with a funnel high spout of icy water drenching the decks. In seconds, with a list of 17 degrees, *Edinburgh* slumped to a stop settling deeper into the water.

Already there were other sounds; the noise of things breaking adrift, sliding along the steepening decks. The turret was still firing when the torpedo struck. The young gunnery officer, directing the fall of shot from the turret top, was ejected through the hatch on to the roof. Here, by clinging to a finger-width ledge he managed to save himself from being thrown to the deck below. It was a tricky moment but clambering back he resumed gunfire control as though nothing had happened.

As damage control reports from below reached the bridge it was clear that the ship was open from side to side with the sea washing straight through. It was also clear that the outer strakes of the upper deck and possibly bits of the hull were the only things that were holding the ship together. The admiral, aware that she might break in two at any moment and sink with severe loss of life gave the order, 'Abandon ship'. At the same time he signalled the minesweepers to come alongside to take off the wounded, passengers and the crew.

Below decks another battle raged; one for survival. When the torpedo hit one of the lower messdecks had a number of men passing through it and the explosion ruptured adjacent bulkheads and oil tanks. Nineteen year-old Able Seaman William Wallis who was in that messdeck described what happened.

It was just like being in a bad car crash. All the lights went out and we were left in darkness – a blackness that defied description. Amid the deafening roar of scalding steam erupting from burst steam pipes, thick fuel oil spurted in all directions from a dozen or more fractures enveloping us in its filthy black slime. In trying to breathe we found we were swallowing the stuff. In the blackness, trying to feel our way we kept losing direction. Our one hope was to find the ladder and by clearing the lockers I eventually managed to find it. But I had a man with a broken leg hanging around my neck and as I tried to climb the ladder he was slipping from me. The ladder was also covered in oil and I couldn't get a proper grip. I managed to hold him on to me, pulling him up and out towards a glimmer of light coming from a gangway somewhere high above. I could hear them screaming down below, 'Help me – help me'.

By this time, my eyes were getting used to the darkness and I went down again. At the bottom of the ladder they were fighting to get up. I managed to grab one man and it turned out to be a pal of mine. Coated in the black oil however you couldn't tell one man from another. By this time I had to get out because my lungs were bursting with the smell and having swallowed some I was vomiting. After a few minutes I went down to the hatch again to see if I could do anything, only to discover that the heavy cover had fallen down with the listing and had jammed shut. I got some help but although we tried, we couldn't move it. They were still screaming when we left.

I remember hearing the hoarse cries of one man in particular. He was from our mess, a real tough guy and a bully; everybody was afraid of him, he made life a misery. He had no regard for man, no respect for God. But at that moment, facing eternity, he became a gibbering infant, screaming and crying for the Lord to help him. He died with the rest down there.

But we had to go as the list was increasing. We went up on deck and found that one of the minesweepers had come alongside and was already taking the wounded and passengers aboard. While we waited our turn, we huddled together behind the hangar out of the freezing wind. We were all in pretty bad shape and I went across to the wardroom to find a cloth to wipe the oil from our eyes. There was a door open near the wardroom leading into the Major of Marine's cabin. On the bed lay a clean white sheet and pulling it away I ripped it up for some of the others to have a piece each. My shoes at this time were squelching with oil and seeing a pair of tapered shoes sticking out under the bunk, I grabbed them and put them on and wore them all the time I was in Russia. I went back to wipe my pal's eyes and the back of his neck and as I did so the flesh came off with the oil. He must have caught the full force of one of the steam bursts.

One of the radar ratings Harry Cook, who had a miraculous escape, recounted his story.

There were eight of us in this lower compartment when the torpedo hit. The deck plating above us, yielding under the pressure of the explosion jammed the hatch cover. In charge of us was a long-term petty officer who treated us with contempt. He despised us not only because we were young and inexperienced but principally because we were 'hostilities only'. We all shouted and battered at the hatch but no one heard us. Eventually, by exerting all our combined strength against the cover, we managed to move it open just wide enough to allow the petty officer to force his body through the gap and slide out. We were all very young and very frightened and the tension was terrible. We waited there in the dark for an hour assuring ourselves that the PO would soon be bringing help. But still no one came. We tried the telephone but could get no reply. After what seemd an eternity the phone actually rang. It was from Damage Control. The voice said – 'We didn't know you were down there – we thought you were all out. We saw the petty officer who came barging up the ladder and when we asked, "Is everybody out?", he replied "Yes". As a result we locked the upper hatch cover in the deck above'. Very soon a Damage Control party arrived and forced the cover and in moments we were free. You can imagine how we felt. In fact if we could have found that PO at the time, I think we would have half-killed him. By his deliberate neglect we could have all died.

Icing on the upper deck. Chipping off ice was an important duty for the ship's company in these waters

HMS *Edinburgh* foreground with *Sheffield* and *Kenya*

A convoy to Russia under attack

Part of the dockyard at Rosta in the Kola inlet. The building in the foreground is the communal latrine

Town-class cruisers carried a Walrus aircraft seen being launched by catapult

Captain Faulkner (*left*) and Rear-Admiral Bonham-Carter

The German destroyer *Hermann Schoemann* on fire and sinking

HMS Edinburgh looking aft. Part of the quarter-deck can be seen falling away at the moment when the oxyacetylene burners have done their work

As the ship's list increased it was found that the 6-inch guns were unable to bear on target but the smaller armament still continued their barrage of fire. Soon shellfire from the enemy became sporadic and the two active destroyers were observed taking the crew off the damaged ship. As Captain Faulkner watched the Germans retire he must have raised a prayer of thanksgiving, for as he said later, 'I shall never understand why they didn't come in and finish us off. I think they had acknowledged defeat after being so heavily shot at.'

With the minesweeper *Harrier* secured along the port side and *Gossamer* starboard, the loading of the wounded and passengers began. The transfer of wounded from a sloping deck on a higher level to the decks of *Harrier* was a formidable undertaking. Time was the essence with the ship almost in two and likely to break up at any moment. Most of the wounded were on stretchers and had to be lifted over the side of the listing ship and lowered by whatever means available. The deck of *Harrier* was at least 12 feet below that of *Edinburgh*'s and the transfer was made more tricky by the lifting and falling swell. One by one the stretcher cases were lowered as carefully as possible but almost inevitably there were accidents. A few became dislodged from their stretchers and crashed to the decks below. Others, almost naked from their sick bay beds fell over the side and became entangled in the scrambling nets, nearly freezing to death in the Arctic wind.

Following the wounded came the passengers, nearly 200 of them. Many were Poles, released from Russian prisoner-of-war camps and thankful to be in the hands of the British. Among those who died in *Edinburgh* was General Sikorski's secretary who had been killed in his bunk in the earlier torpedo explosion astern. Apart from these there were a number of British army and Royal Air Force personnel. All instructors, they had been in Russia training the Russians in the use of British tanks and Hurricane planes. In addition there were many Czechs who had escaped from their country when Hitler ravaged it, had been interned in Russia and were now being sent to England. A deal of commotion arose over these. They were shouting and pleading they did not want to be sent back to Russia again after three years of confinement. Only after being given an assurance that on arrival at Murmansk they would be transferred as soon as possible to a ship returning to England was calm restored.

Then followed the major operation of transferring about 800 men to the minesweepers *Harrier* (Captain E. P. Hinton, DSO, RN) and *Gossamer* (Lieut-Commander T. C. Crease), each embarking about 400. Captain Hinton and his crew showed remarkable calmness for the minesweeper was in danger of being crushed as *Edinburgh* increased her list. He signalled to Captain Faulkner, 'You are leaning on me rather heavily'. Meanwhile, the Russian tug *Rubin* came racing in towards *Harrier* and for some obscure reason misjudged her speed and collided with a resounding crack. Fortunately little damage was done to either vessel. While the transfer was going on, someone asked, 'What about the gold?' The question brought an answer which is unprintable. Still snug in the lower region of the cruiser lay the mass of gold bullion covered deep in sea water.

Aboard both minesweepers the decks were becoming so overcrowded there was imminent danger of the vessels capsizing. Although the men were asked to go below to stabilise the vessel a large number were reluctant to do so. It was understandable in the circumstances, especially for those who had recently been trapped below decks in *Edinburgh*. Aware of the danger *Edinburgh*'s first lieutenant, Lieut-Commander Arthur Fitzroy-Talbot, later to become Vice-Admiral Sir Arthur Fitzroy-Talbot, KBE, CB, DSO and Bar, DL, RN, and subsequently Commander-in-Chief, Plymouth, called on the men to follow him and led the way as far down as it was possible to go. With the extra 400 men aboard each vessel they were now packed like sardines.

Uppermost in everyone's mind must have been the thought 'What happens if we get torpedoed now?' Finally the admiral and Captain Faulkner took their departure for the last time. There was nothing more that could be done. Officers and men had acted with outstanding courage and determination. As Captain Faulkner later said of their ordeal, 'Emergencies were met with such calmness and confidence they ceased to be emergencies'.

The lines were let go and the two minesweepers with *Foresight* and *Forester* stood off to watch *Edinburgh* go down. Contrary to all expectations, however, she did not continue to heel over and measures were taken to hasten her end. The admiral decided she should be sunk by gunfire. *Harrier* therefore fired twenty rounds of semi-armour piercing shells into her with little obvious effect except that two fires were started. Two patterns of depth charges were then dropped close alongside but this was also unsuccessful.

A breakdown in communications at this point nearly produced a panic situation below decks in the mine-sweepers. No one had thought of informing the tightly packed survivors that efforts were to be made to sink *Edinburgh*. When the explosions of shells and depth charges reverberated through the hulls of the ships like the metallic clanging of a great sledge hammer, they naturally thought they were being attacked again and would all be drowned like rats in a trap. It was only by the reassuring message passed down from the men above decks that their fears were allayed.

Finally *Foresight* was ordered to fire her one remaining torpedo. From the decks of the circling ships, officers and men watched in silence. The great ship for which they had fought and bled and for which men had died was now to be lost for ever. As the lever went over the long steel torpedo carrying its lethal warhead, the final executioner of *Edinburgh*, leapt from the destroyer to speed on its way to the target. Those last few seconds a breathless hush of despair hung over the stretch of grey sea between the two ships. Then it was there, plunging deep into the vitals of the cruiser with a booming explosion. A sheet of flame rose high, fingering skywards, mushrooming into a pillar of black smoke. Silently at first, slowly, almost reluctantly, she rolled over on her side, then in an agony of tearing, rending metal the fore part broke away. The stern disappeared quickly but the bows rising high stayed poised for a moment, then in a tumult of bubbling, gurgling water, disappeared. With it came the smell of oil fuel. A smell they had got used to in recent days. An obscene disgusting stench that persisted, lingering on the freezing water of the Barents Sea.

As *Edinburgh* disappeared she bore within her hull the bodies of fifty-seven men. Almost at the same moment the *Hermann Schoemann* was settling into her last resting place on the floor of the ocean with the bodies of those killed aboard her.

Aboard *Harrier* the log recorded *Edinburgh* as sinking in position 71–51 degrees north, 35–10 degrees east. The time 9 a.m. The date 2 May 1942.

There was a final look at the pool of oil and wreckage littering the surface over *Edinburgh*'s grave as minesweepers and destroyers moved away. As speed increased, hulls began to vibrate, halyards shook and rattled in the wind of their advance and the grey bows slicing into the icy water plumed back their curling waves, showing brilliant white against the dark waters of the Arctic Ocean. It was time to make for the Kola inlet.

As the morning wore on, the two forces withdrew at speed, the Germans towards Kirkenes, the British to Murmansk, each leaving their dead and carrying the dying and wounded. Both sides had lost a ship and despite the difference in tonnage each was as important to the one as to the other. It had been a furious naval engagement in which there had been neither victor nor vanquished, neither winner nor loser.

At ten o'clock that morning, as bleak icy winds swept over the waters above *Edinburgh*'s resting place and with no ship visible from horizon to horizon, the black shiny hull of U boat *456* surfaced amongst the floating wreckage. From the hatch emerged Lieutenant Max Teichert, the man initially responsible for *Edinburgh*'s destruction. The German High Command was still unaware that the cruiser had been sunk, which was only confirmed when Teichert returned to base. During the heavy engagement between the two forces, the lieutenant had positioned himself close to the cruiser but over forty feet deep so as not to endanger his boat. He had heard the detonation of the torpedo that hit *Edinburgh* and at about 9 a.m., the familiar sounds of a large ship sinking. He later reported, 'She was so near, we were all afraid she would fall on top of us.' As he surveyed the scene there was no further doubt that the cruiser had sunk. A large oil slick covered the immediate area and encased within its glutinous mass floated caps and chairs, papers and uniforms. Amidst the flotsam in incongruous relief scores of white tropical helmets bobbed about in a macabre dance to the rhythmic motion of the waves. With a sigh of satisfaction, Teichert returned to the U boat and ordered a course for home, knowing he could claim a major success in the war against the British.

Three days later on 5 May, the British Admiralty announced the loss of *Edinburgh*, and of a second ship, a destroyer. In this case, however, the Germans had not been responsible. On 1 May, the battleship *King George V* while providing distant cover, rammed and sank the British destroyer *Punjabi* in dense fog and forced her under water. As the *Punjabi* went down her depth charges detonated beneath the battleship's hull and *King George V* was so damaged she had to be docked for repairs. It was another blow against the Allies in a year when the tide of adversity flowed so strongly against them.

Throughout 2 May, *Foresight* and *Forester* accompanied by the minesweepers moved steadily towards North Russia.

From time to time the two destroyers had to stop to correct engine failures but by arrangement late that evening they slowed to close one another. Side by side on the decks lay the bodies of those killed in action. One by one in neatly parcelled shrouds of canvas, the bodies were lifted on to the tilting boards covered by Union Jacks on which flurries of snowflakes fell in silent tribute. As the brief service was read, fragmented by the wind, pipes shrilled, the planks tipped sharply and the weighted shrouds slid from under the flag to disappear over the side.

Early the following morning the little group of ships entered the Kola inlet where the crew were disembarked, some at Polyarnoe, some at Vaenga and the wounded at Murmansk. The minesweepers, arriving at Vaenga half way up the inlet, had to stop to refuel from the Russians. There was no interpreter and one of *Harrier*'s officers Lieutenant Christopher McLean was brought a paper to sign as a receipt for the oil. This he did but the Russian official was dissatisfied and by signs made it clear that he must have a rubber stamp. Very tired and with somewhat frayed nerves from the last three days' ordeal, McLean took the only rubber stamp then available bearing the word 'Cancelled' and stamped the receipt. The Russian went away happy.

Soon after arriving at Murmansk, *Harrier*'s commanding officer Captain Hinton received the following letter, quoted verbatim, from the captain of the Russian tug *Rubin* which had earlier rammed him.

Dear Sir,

Soviet's seaman was witness of heroic battle English seamen with predominants powers of enemy. English seamen did observe their sacred duty before Fatherland. We are prouding to staunchness and courage of English seamens – our Allies. I am very sorry what injured your ship by approach to board for what I must to beg pardon

Commander of Division

It was a letter which was greatly appreciated by everyone.

Disembarking at Murmansk, Admiral Bonham-Carter sent the following message to the captain and crew of *Harrier*.

> ... it was inspiring to see the minesweepers staying on the scene of action and taking every opportunity of firing at the enemy when visibility permitted. The manner in which *Harrier* and *Gossamer* were brought alongside the listing *Edinburgh* during the action showed a fine feat of seamanship and I fully confirm the Commanding Officer of *Edinburgh*'s report of the way we were treated on board. Never have I seen more kindness and attention than was given to myself, Captain, officers and men than by the Captain, officers and ship's company of *Harrier* in which we left.

He later dispatched the following report to the Commander-in-Chief of the Home Fleet, Admiral Sir John Tovey.

> When the third torpedo hit *Edinburgh* on the port side just before the catapult and practically opposite the place where the first torpedo had struck on the starboard side, I realised that the ship must be open from side to side and this was later confirmed by reports from below.
>
> I considered that she might break in two at any moment and sink and as the ship was slowly settling, I instructed the Captain to 'abandon ship'. It was with great reluctance that the order was given entirely on my own responsibility. I felt it was quite impossible to save her. I have since spent many hours thinking over this decision and am still convinced that it was the only possible step to take and if placed in the same position again I should give the same order. Had I kept men on board any longer many valuable lives would certainly have been lost.
>
> I cannot understand the behaviour of the German destroyers unless as stated in the report of the Senior

Officer of the 6th Minesweeper Flotilla, they mistook the minesweepers for destroyers and did not realise the condition *Edinburgh* was in. If they had shown any real determination I consider that not only *Edinburgh* but possibly all ships present could have been sunk.

When *Edinburgh* was finally abandoned there were not many enemy ships in sight and although gunfire was heard later after I embarked in *Harrier* they were not seen again. It is probable therefore they were not aware that the ship was actually sunk and it is possible they did not realise that one of their torpedoes had hit.

I cannot speak too highly of the behaviour of the Captain, officers and men of *Edinburgh* from the time she was first torpedoed. The coolness, calmness and cheerfulness shown by the Captain was felt right throughout the ship and at no time was there any sign of depression through the intense cold and lack of sleep nor loss of heart despite the knowledge that surface, submarine and air attack was imminent.

The way in which *Foresight* and *Forester* went into attack superior forces and the manner in which they were handled could not have been more gallant.

I would like to place on record my deep appreciation for all that has been done for us by the Senior Based Naval Officer at Murmansk and his staff under the most difficult circumstances with inadequate facilities. Over 1000 survivors from *Edinburgh* and other ships have been housed, fed and where necessary clothed and their individual kindness will never be forgotten.

Edinburgh finally sank in 71-51 N. 35-10 E.

It is no doubt fully realised how deeply I regret the loss of so fine a cruiser but I hope it will be appreciated that I alone was responsible for the movement of *Edinburgh* and that in no way can any criticism be levelled at Captain Faulkner who I hope will be given another sea command as early as possible.

> Rear-Admiral commanding 18th Cruiser
> Squadron
>   Rear-Admiral Stuart Bonham-Carter

A day or two after arriving in the Kola inlet, *Harrier* entertained Rear-Admiral Bonham-Carter in the small wardroom. Christopher McLean recalls that at the end of the evening he thanked them very much for their hospitality and for all the help they had given in the *Edinburgh* action. He had no way of reciprocating but wondered whether they had ever seen an admiral stand on his head. This he proceeded to do much to the delight and astonishment of his audience.

The survivors of *Edinburgh* who came ashore at Polyarnoe and Vaenga did so with mixed feelings. On the one hand, thankfulness they were alive but on the other a sense of despondency at the unbelievable desolation of the Russian coast. Most were under the impression that in a few days they would be aboard ships returning to the United Kingdom. Sadly this was a false conception, for in the weeks and months that followed they were to endure discomfort, cold, hunger and many privations before returning to England. Indeed many of them who had survived the *Edinburgh* sinking were to die in the several attempts to reach home.

The World War in 1942 was heading to a climax with the Allies reeling under severe losses and gaining few successes. Britain had lost three of her great battleships, *Prince of Wales, Repulse* and *Hood*, and America had sustained a terrible defeat at the hands of the Japanese by the annihilation of over half their fleet at Pearl Harbour. Although this had brought the United States into the war she applied her naval and military strength in an effort to defeat the Japanese in the Pacific theatre.

In the Atlantic and the Arctic Oceans German U boats were gaining overwhelming predominance with ruthless energy. More and more U boats were being built and launched at the alarming rate of five each week. They could now station over 100 submarines along the convoy routes, sinking thousands of tons of Allied shipping. Despite the resolute efforts of escort ships many merchant vessels were sent to the bottom every month. Although some Allied successes could be claimed the balance was to the advantage of the enemy and much was to happen before the tide turned.

CHAPTER 9

Survivors Face Life in Russia

IT WAS NEARLY 10 O'CLOCK on the night of 2 May when the minesweepers drew alongside the wooden jetty at Polyarnoe, a small settlement on the western bank of the Kola inlet, to disembark the *Edinburgh* survivors. A watery sun filtering through the grey daylight, almost obscured at times by light snow showers, greeted their arrival. It was a comfortless welcome as they surveyed the desolate snow wastes stretching away to distant pine forests. Carrying the few things they had, the men filed off the ships and mustered on the snow-covered banks of the shoreline. They gazed out on a land which by its very character seemed to discharge an aura of hostility. A land without a soul, cold in its nature, frigid in reception.

Untidy and in disarray, crude wooden huts stood out starkly against the white snow in their isolation. Thousands of timber spars and planking lay strewn everywhere, left to rot. A rickety wooden shack leaning crazily and looking as though it might heel over at any moment, proved to be the dockyard toilet built over the tidal river. A few Russian men and women dressed in voluminous layers of clothing moved around at a distance, watching suspiciously. Some wore uncured skin coats alive with maggots. The survivors looked anything but a smartly turned out ship's company. All they had were the clothes they stood up in. Some had managed to grab a few personal belongings before they abandoned ship but these were very few. Some, especially stokers and engine room staff, had no time to gather warm clothing. Trousers and singlet, with a blanket around their shoulders, was all they had to protect them from the bitter wind.

The demands of the last few days had taken its toll. The hours closed up at action stations, the nerve-breaking tension, the loss of sleep, the makeshift meals of cocoa and corned-beef sandwiches, living under a cloud of recurring anxieties, all these things had shredded their resistance. There had been few moments since the first torpedo had plunged into the ship when they could forget the dangers lurking in the grey-black waters around them. There had been no moments of relaxation when they could lay aside their worries and find peace of mind. Now with the tension gone an almost unbelievable weariness had taken its place. More tired than they had ever been, filthy, oil-soaked, unshaven, shivering in the sub-zero temperature, they waited, wondering what was to become of them. And yet morale could not have been higher. The moral fibre which had brought them through so far now bonded them even closer and in adversity companionship became the very bulwark of resistance. Yet deep in every heart and mind lingered a chilling thought; a disquiet which no man dare give words to. One day, perhaps tomorrow, perhaps in a few weeks, they would embark for the United Kingdom in another ship, and out there beyond the Kola inlet the enemy would be waiting. First would come the Condor reconnaisance planes casually circling the convoy like great vultures, then the U boats, threading across the convoy route with their deadly torpedoes, waiting for the kill. And inevitably, there would be the dive-bombers screaming out of a sky of persistent daylight. No matter how far north the ships sought protection the bombers would find them, choosing the time and place to kill, and kill and kill again.

But now they found comfort in one another's companionship, recounting their experiences over the last few hours and days. Unfounded predictions as to their future were rampant. Absurd rumours passed from one to another like wildfire. A seaman claimed he knew one of the stokers who was friendly with one of the chief ERAs, who had overheard the commander say that Winston Churchill himself had given orders for the battleship *King George V* to sail to Murmansk to pick up the ship's company and bring them home. Another knew one of the stewards in the wardroom who had overheard a conversation between two officers that they were all to be transported by train across Russia to Siberia and on to Vladivostok, and from there through the Pacific to the UK. These and other equally outrageous buzzes were brought to a stop by the stentorian voice of the master-at-arms calling them together. As the lean figure of Captain Faulkner climbed a little wearily on to a sharply rising piece of ground nearby, the men gathered around. His face looked tired in the cold light of the Arctic night. It was not a time for long speeches. It was, however, an opportunity to congratulate them on the courageous way in which they had defended the ship and all they had done to try to save it. With a trace of emotion in his voice he told them this would probably be the last time they would be altogether as a ship's company for they were to be divided into two groups. One to stay at Polyarnoe and the other to re-embark on *Gossamer* and be taken up river to Vaenga, while the sick and wounded would be transferred to Murmansk. They would have to stay in camps provided by the Russians until they could be transferred in small groups to ships going home. While the naval base officers would do everything possible to supply their needs they were entirely in the hands of the Russians, who themselves were living in sub-human conditions. There would be many privations to endure but how long they would be kept in Russia it was impossible to say. Then wishing them 'Good luck', he saluted and walked away.

There was a stunned silence as the men digested the news. It seemed impossible to believe that after the long period of close association from their commissioning three years ago they were soon to be separated. It had always been a happy ship's company and few had considered the possibility of sudden fragmentation. If ever they arrived back in the UK, and it was a big if, they would be drafted in ones and twos to other ships and to other parts of the world, probably never to meet again. It was a sobering thought.

Then came the roll call by which they knew officially who had been lost in the two actions. As names were called, the men answered but for fifty-seven of those names there was no response. Only a silence, alive with the memory of the face, the voice, perhaps an incident when they were last seen alive. The crew had been together for those three long years, living with one another, working with one another, exchanging personal confidences. It was a period when friendship and comradeship grew into a natural bond. Hidden in the ranks, tough, strong hard-swearing men wept quietly as the names of their closest friends remained unanswered.

But for everyone there was concern for wives, children, parents or sweethearts at home. Notification to next-of-kin of those killed in action became a constant problem for the naval authorities. To announce to the nation that a British ship had been sunk without first notifying the nearest relative meant unnecessary mental anguish for thousands of people. The usual procedure was to inform next-of-kin before releasing the name of the ship to the public. Sometimes this was not possible. Often as not the German propaganda machine, through the notorious announcer Lord Haw-Haw, would gleefully inform the British people of a sinking within an hour or two of the event, frequently with exaggerated claims of their success. In these circumstances, the Government had no alternative but to confirm the sinking through the radio or national newspapers with the closing announcement, 'The next of kin will be informed'. These words brought a time of crushing anxiety for those at home. Through many a window anxious eyes watched the approach of the postman delivering mail down through the street. Every rat-a-tat of the letter box set the heart pounding. Would it be the dreaded telegram bearing the words, 'The Admiralty regrets to inform you ...'? It was therefore with much relief that the men were assured everything possible was being done to inform those at home of their safety.

After a brief farewell to the group re-embarking for Vaenga, the four hundred men destined for the Polyarnoe camp began the long march through deep snow, in their condition a weary business. Here and there in isolation a few wooden houses revealed tall chimneys through banks of snow piled high from the last fall. Nearby, a beaten road leading in the direction of Murmansk, bestrewed with large pot-holes and bumps, carried heavy army lorries heaving and plunging in the mud and slush of the worn track.

Hungry and tired, the men eventually arrived at the settlement which turned out to be an area of large wooden structures sited at the top of a steep hill. Inside, running down the 150 feet length of each building were two long platforms with a second staging above, both about 14 feet wide, floored by wide wooden slats on which rested mattresses filled with crushed pine needles. To accommodate 350 men in each hut, they had to sleep head to head, and of course in their own clothes. Each man was issued with a towel but despite the sub-zero temperatures only one sleeping blanket could be provided.

None of them had had a hot meal since leaving the Kola inlet on 28 April and they looked forward to something substantial to fill their empty bellies. To their astonishment they were told they could not be fed here. Having staked their claim to a mattress, they were again regrouped and marched off to an eating house at Polyarny, a village another two miles away. The eating house turned out to be a large wooden shed with tables and wooden benches. The hot meal to which they had so looked forward was not forthcoming. Instead, they were issued with an enamel bowl and a spoon roughly hand-carved from wood and given an evil-smelling gruel made from fish, a slice of black bread green with mildew, and a beaker of pine-needle tea, a liquid concocted from pouring boiling water on to bruised pine needles.

It was indeed a setback to the ship's company and many of the men despite their hunger couldn't get the stuff down. Those who did found that by the time they had walked the two miles back to sleeping quarters they were hungrier than when they had begun. Almost inevitably there followed complaints, bitter complaints, from men who were hearty eaters and now found themselves on a diet which was to them starvation level. On that first day many declared they had no intention of eating such muck but after a couple of days their hunger was such they ate anything put before them. As the days passed most found their stamina running low and the walk through the snow to reach the dining hall utterly exhausting. They lost weight rapidly and by the end of their stay in North Russia some of the men were down to a mere six stones.

The billets themselves were in a disgusting state, ankle deep in filth and alive with mice which swarmed over the men as they lay in their bunks at night. Cleaning gear was borrowed from visiting ships and with typical naval thoroughness they set to, sweeping out and scrubbing the quarters to make them reasonably habitable. As the days passed physical training programmes were arranged. Efforts were made to provide entertainment and even a football match arranged, although so fit were the Russians and so proficient that the *Edinburgh* team was completely out-classed. PT sessions were held on a nearby frozen lake each morning until one of the class fell through the ice and was barely rescued from drowning. From then on all exercises were carried out on terra firma. A sports gala was held on one occasion attended by Captain Faulkner who at the close said with a smile, 'This has been so successful, I think we shall have to make it into an annual event.' Although every effort was made by the captain and Paymaster-Commander E. F. B. George to improve the food situation there was little room for negotiation. The Russians in Murmansk were in just as sorry a state as the British. The authorities provided what they could but with supplies frequently unable to get through on the rail lifeline to Murmansk there was little that could be done.

The front line was only twenty miles away and frequently the sky was lit with gun flashes as heavy artillery bombardments took place. Almost every day German planes flew over bombing and machine-gunning everything they could see and on occasions the buildings were riddled with bullets from attacking aircraft. But by the time the Luftwaffe were fully engaged in the raids, Russian fighters were in the air intercepting their return and it became a daily routine for the camp to turn out to watch the dog fights overhead.

The railway line had become the vital link in the bitter war which waged around the railhead and port of Murmansk and southwards along the Finnish border. The track not only brought much needed food and other supplies to the hard-pressed Russian armies defending the port but allowed the transport of vital war materials brought into the Kola inlet by British and American convoy ships to be sent south to support the Russian armies fighting with their backs to the gates of Moscow and to front-line Leningrad.

Leningrad, situated on the coast of the Gulf of Finland, was one of the two cities which Hitler was determined to capture, the other being Moscow. As the Germans drove east the city was besieged. The inhabitants fought bravely and with dogged determination in the streets of the suburbs, and in spite of lack of ammunition and food successfully defended it. Although 700,000 of the population were starved, killed or frozen to death, the beleaguered city withstood its gruesome siege of twenty-eight months and never fell into German hands.

The Murmansk railway was in fact the key to the situation and aware of this, the Germans decided to cut the line, thereby terminating convoy supplies. Although Archangel, 300 miles to the east, was a well protected and useful port it was entirely frozen up in winter and ships could only enter with the aid of ice-breakers, a slow and entirely impracticable business. The railway line was a single track carrying thousands of tons of war material, far in excess of the original purpose for which it had been designed. Later in the war supplies flowed into Russia through Persia and the backdoor port of Vladivostok but at this time the bulk was transported through the Arctic route to North Russia. The massive weight and volume of war materials sent to the USSR by America and Britain may be judged from the following figures.

War equipment shipped to Russia

By the United States:

14,795 aircraft, 7500 tanks, 51,000 jeeps, 35,000 motor cycles, 8000 tractors, 376,000 trucks, 8000 anti-aircraft guns, 132,000 sub-machine guns, 345,000 tons of explosives, 2000 locomotives, 11,000 flat cars and wagons, 49,000 tons of leather, 15,000,000 pairs of boots, 3,786,000 tyres, 842,000 tons of chemicals, 2,670,000 tons of petrol, 1,050,000 miles of field telephone cable, food shipments to the value of 1,312,000,000 dollars.

Total value 11,260,343,600 dollars.

By Britain:

7400 aircraft (of which 3000 from USA), 5200 tanks (of which 1390 from Canada), 5000 anti-tank guns, 4000 rifles and machine guns, 1800 sets of radar equipment, 4000 sets of radio equipment, 2000 telephone sets, 472,000,000 projectiles, 4 submarines, 9 motor torpedo boats, 14 minesweepers.

Total value £308,000,000.

In addition, foodstuffs, machinery, industrial plant, medical supplies and hospital equipment were sent to the value of £120,000,000.

The railway runs across the Kola peninsula for 150 miles, verging a multitude of lakes dominating the landscape there and bringing it to the port of Kandalaksha at the western extremity of the White Sea. This in itself was a most vulnerable piece of rail track running as it does between the natural border of the sea and the Finnish frontier only 50 miles to the west. From here the line is maintained for another 250 miles, running south-east along the southern coast of the White Sea to Belomorsk, where it turns south for 500 miles parallel to the Finnish border at a distance of 150 miles. The stretch of line, much threatened, running between the great lakes of Onega and Ladoga was known as the Karelian front. The line then normally ended in the Leningrad area where trains could be re-routed to their final terminals along any of the tracks radiating from there.

In 1941, the Finns succeeded in cutting the railway line in the neighbourhood of Lake Onega. Anticipating this, the Russians had begun constructing a loop line running east from Belomorsk to join the Archangel–Moscow line, thereby reducing the risk to supplies passing through the Karelian front area. After incredible efforts on the part of engineering and rail construction gangs and notwithstanding the deplorable conditions experienced on the coast of the White Sea in winter, the loop line was opened in a very short time and once more supply trains travelled south with their precious freights.

One of the most significant sources of raw material for Germany was the rich nickel ore mining area of Petsamo on the Barents Sea coast of Northern Finland, not far from

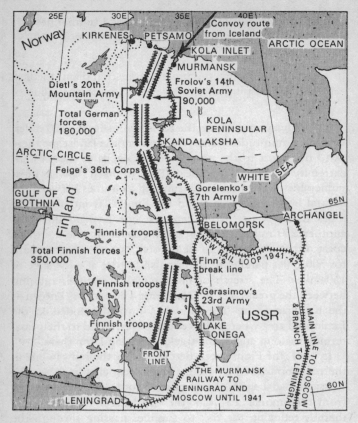

The battle for the vital Murmansk railway showing
disposition of armies.

Murmansk. Ships carrying the ore operated a shuttle service
around North Cape, then south down to German ports
along the Norwegian coast but this traffic was harassed by
British submarines which were able to sink many of the
vessels. Thus the Petsamo nickel ore with Swedish iron ore,

used in the manufacture of munitions, became a vital part of the German war effort and the supply had to be maintained whatever the cost.

By occupying Norway and Denmark the Germans secured both the Baltic and their northern flank and by this means improved the safety of the ore traffic. The Führer, however, still feared an Allied invasion of Norway leading to a bridge with Russia in the north. If this happened Germany would certainly lose the Petsamo mines. As a consequence he formed the Army of Lapland, later to be known as the German 20th Mountain Army. These 180,000 troops were under the command of General Dietl, who was charged with holding the Petsamo area and fighting alongside his ally Finland which had been at war with Russia since 1939. With the introduction of convoys to North Russia the resistance of the Russian armies had stiffened so that the German advances along the eastern front had been reduced. But while Hitler was doing everything in his power to stop the convoys getting through to Murmansk he also had to cut the rail link and the span of track in the Kandalaksha area was the place to do it.

Early in December 1940, operational plans had been produced. Again Hitler overruled his General Staff and ordered Dietl to take Murmansk, secure the whole of the Kola peninsula and cut the vital rail line as well. If this was successful, the operation known as 'Silver Fox' would not only terminate the flow of Allied aid but could possibly be the start of an outflanking movement round the Russian armies further south. On paper it looked a simple task as the German and Finnish forces together outnumbered the USSR forces by two to one. But wars are not fought on paper and the three separate German thrusts eastward were a failure. The Russian units although outnumbered had the advantages of strong artillery, short lines of communication and well prepared defensive positions.

On the German side the weakness of their strategy lay in

poor communication and supply. There were very few roads and in some areas pack mules had to be used to supply the troops. In the spring of 1942, while *Edinburgh* survivors were at Polyarnoe and Vaenga, the northern battle was reaching a climax. At that time, the 14th Soviet Army under the command of General Frolov held the northern sector which included the approaches to Murmansk and the Kola peninsula. In the previous June Frolov had only two rifle divisions and a hastily formed third, made up of civilians and sailors. These were thrown into the defence of the port and by a courageous stand were enough to stop the Germans a few miles from the town. By the following April–May, he was strong enough to attack Petsamo with units of the Russian Navy supporting him. The attack, however, was repulsed and apart from local actions on either side the front remained static.

If the Germans had succeeded in cutting the railway line at Kandalaksha and capturing the Kola peninsular the convoys would have had to be diverted to Archangel. This would virtually have brought an end to convoys to North Russia as a vast armada of ships would have had to be convoyed through in a very short space of time, with the prospect of a further 300 miles of attack by submarines and aircraft. The rail link remained a frequent target. Supply trains and the track itself were constantly attacked by the Luftwaffe, destroying locomotives, wrecking trains and smashing the permanent way. But the Russian repair gangs, working round the clock, restored the line as soon as damage was inflicted and kept supplies rolling south.

As retaliation, Russian fighter aircraft flew regular patrols from the airfield at Vaenga whenever the weather and the state of the runway permitted. Vaenga was an unusual airfield with its long narrow cutting through pine forests. The hangars were rough sheds beneath trees, each side of the dirt runway. Dozens of RAF personnel spent long months at this bleak station instructing the Russians how to fly and maintain the Hurricanes operating from there. Some of the Russian women were engaged in active combat, flying Stormoviks and Yaks in fighter patrols against the Stukas and Junkers 88s. It was rumoured that some deliberately crashed their aircraft into approaching waves of German bombers when they ran out of ammunition. They were well liberated, drinking Red Army vodka straight from the bottle like men, and rolling coarse grained 'mahorka' tobacco in dated issues of *Pravda* to make cigarettes by twisting the ends.

As the intensity of the war on the Finnish border and attacks on the supply line increased, so the food situation became more critical. The Russian soldiers were worse off than the navy survivors at times. As they returned from the front line, the many casualties were sent to hospital but the remainder were billeted in the same hut area as the *Edinburgh* men. They were glad of anything the British could let them have from their meagre ration. No one could justifiably complain; supplies of food were simply not available.

With the rail line often cut, the crew supplied what they could from their limited stocks. Despite the language barrier a developing fraternisation emerged between the two sides, and from the survivors a tremendous respect for the Russians in their singleness of purpose. Even in those dark days when the tide of war was running against the Allies it was thought that the Germans would lose because the Russians simply would not be beaten.

British destroyers, paying brief visits to the port between convoys, did what they could for the *Edinburgh* men. Occasionally invitations were extended for a number to come down to the ship and have a meal, perhaps a bath. Sometimes a small party of the survivors would return with a tin of corned beef or a small piece of cheese. No one kept anything for themselves. It was made up into a communal pot of unusual stew. If the destroyer's food supply would allow they might bring back a few potatoes, to be rationed out one per man per day for a limited period.

A concession the Russians made which was gratefully accepted was the use of the communal bath house. It proved to be a surprising and highly amusing business. Men and women shared the same facilities. Once inside the large building everyone queued up at one end. They then had to undress and hand over their clothes to Russian women attendants, who laundered them while they were bathing and issued the bathers with clean underwear on the way out. An old woman was the caretaker and any banter or horseplay from the men would be rewarded by the old lady chasing them around the building with a brush, smacking them across their bottoms. The hot water was a great treat but the soap like cement. The old navy soap which so many had grumbled about on the ship was beautiful by comparison.

After a few days at the camps news came that permission had been granted for men to get a shave at the submarine base nearby. Money was easy to come by as the Russians had wads of notes and would pay any amount for the most insignificant article, even a British-style cigarette. They would queue up with the Russian sailors for a hair cut or a shave or both. The Russians, who were usually headed for front line service for a spell, would have their heads completely cropped and then shaved 'Yul Brynner style'. For the *Angliski Matroske*, 'Shave – Da – two roubles'. There were two female operatives. One, a large young blonde could well take care of herself and was quite capable of dealing with any ambitious male. She was always smoking. With her cigarette in one hand and wielding a large cut-throat razor in the other she held an advantage no one was prepared to dispute.

Surprisingly, clothing of a sort was reasonably available. The Russians produced oddments of uniform, odd boots and a variety of Russian fur hats. By the time the *Edinburgh* men were fitted out there was little to distinguish them from the Russians. Both the British and Russian authorities were in agreement that boredom through inactivity might prove a growing problem and in this respect the Russians went out of their way to promote various forms of entertainment. A little over a mile down the hill from the quarters at Polyarnoe was a building known as the Red Hall which the survivors were invited to use. The first floor, a war museum, contained captured equipment which had been taken from the Finns on the nearby front, much of it, rather embarrassingly, British. Upstairs provided one room for dancing and another as a sort of theatre. After lengthy negotiations the Russians allowed films to be shown. There were only two, both borrowed by the senior based naval officer Rear-Admiral Robert Bevan, from British warships.

One of the films was a Mickey Mouse and the other *Tales from the Vienna Woods*, which most watched a dozen times or more. Entertainment effort even extended to providing a few dance sessions. Someone had managed to produce an old wind-up gramophone and two records, one a military two-step and the other a tango. The men danced with one another, after some fierce arguments as to whom should lead. Girls were practically non existent but on two occasions a few Russian naval uniformed girls arrived which quickly livened up the situation. Sex starved, the sailors openly exchanged with one another the usual banter about what they would like to do if they could only get the girls into bed. Unfortunately the girls understood English perfectly and representations were made by the Russian naval authorities to curb such lecherous talk. Despite conditions Jack ashore was living up to his reputation.

There was the odd occasion when the Russians provided a three-piece band for a dancing session but the senior Russian commissar who was present would insist on playing the gramophone while the band was playing. A disastrous combination. There was the time when the Russian interpreter came along and suggested a tug-of-war. Could the British find enough big men to take on one of their brigade teams? *Edinburgh* assembled the best they had but when the

Russians turned up they proved to be veritable giants – 6 ft 6 ins tall and built like battleships. The result was a foregone conclusion. Work proved to be one of the best therapeutic occupations. Parties were organised in the unloading and transporting of stores and ammunition. Most of these excursions provided hair-raising experiences, sitting on the top of a lorry load of dynamite, driven at breakneck speed over rough cart tracks by amazons dressed in sombre uniforms and armed with revolvers.

When the *Edinburgh* survivors were offloaded at Polyarnoe and Vaenga, the sick bay staff were of course required to accompany the wounded up river to Murmansk. The hospital there was originally a Russian college. British naval surgeons found the place terribly overcrowded with many casualties arriving daily from the front and these, with the British casualties, had to endure the most primitive medical conditions. British surgeons were not permitted to operate on their own men once they were in Russian hands. They could watch but were not allowed to touch. This attitude on the part of the Russians who would not countenance any interference in their scheduled way of life was difficult to understand. One would have thought that assistance from British surgeons would have relieved the overworked Russian staff. Beds were close together side by side and in addition to the predominantly Russian patients there were men from previous convoys of many colours and nationalities laid out in rows in the corridors.

The operating theatre had six tables and instead of the usual trays for the sterilization of instruments, there were plates and saucers. One of the *Edinburgh* sick bay attendants, Edwin Dennerly, reported.

I saw no anaesthetic machine of any kind and all the Russians had was a solution, sluiced into the wound to deaden it. Operations were going on all the time. The injured had to crawl down the passages towards the operation room passing through a sort of bath wash-house before being admitted. I recall seeing very young female medics doing frontal brain operations. The patients weren't going to survive anyhow. It wasn't so much experimental, as the fact they were doing the best they could with the staff they had.

CHAPTER 10

The Loss of *Trinidad*

FOR THE EDINBURGH SURVIVORS it was a time of waiting, knowing that sooner or later they would have to face the hazards of the voyage homeward. Rather unexpectedly, the first party joined the returning *Trinidad* which left Russia on 13 May. The moment the stricken cruiser in dry dock at Rosta had received the steel plates brought by *Edinburgh* on 19 April, work to repair the extensive damage had gone ahead with feverish haste. Russian women welders were brought in and under the expert eyes and guidance of British construction engineers the plates were jointed and fastened into positions with supporting girders of timber. At best it was a first aid repair. The timber supports were satisfactory while the cruiser lay in dry dock but could not withstand the forces set up in an Arctic storm. Steel was needed.

The problem looked insurmountable to the Royal Naval constructor Commander Hugh Skinner and his staff of shipwrights. Though there were stacks of suitable steel girders in various parts of the yard, they were under the vigilant eyes of Russian sentries and unobtainable. While the Russians were prepared to provide labour for welding jobs they refused to supply steel supports, maintaining these were needed for their own defensive positions in the front line only twenty miles away against the attacking German armies. Surveying all the possibilities the yard could offer, all that could be seen from the decks of *Trinidad* were two small cranes, an old railway locomotive which never moved and a system of rail tracks for it. These went from the dockside, passed under a high wall and out into the periphery of the yard. The leader of the working party, the blacksmith Petty Officer Frank Firth, then came up with an audacious plan which if successful would surely solve the problem. Though they could hardly appropriate and demolish the cranes and the locomotive, railway lines were a very different matter. Cut to the right length they could be easily transported and would make ideal supports for the welded plating. Firstly, the rails would have to be dug out of the track and then cut up. As this had to be done without the knowledge of the sentries a plan was formed. The following day without seeking official approval which they knew would be denied anyway, nor apparently with the blessing of the ship's more senior officers, two parties of ratings inconspicuously left the ship. One party, aptly dubbed the 'Diversionary Squad', was armed with bars of chocolate and the other, the 'Recovery Division', with oxy-acetlyene equipment. Within a few minutes the first group had the complete attention of the sentries, to whom chocolate was like manna from heaven. Almost immediately the 'Recovery Division' set to work. Inside an hour a considerable stretch of the line under the wall had been cut up. Each portion was concealed under sacking until an opportunity arose to bring it furtively aboard. Following this master stroke the ship's artificers welded the lengths of railway line into position to provide the basis for shoring up, which was then supplemented with more timber supports and cement poured into the cavities and recesses to bind everything together. It was as good a job as available materials and facilities would allow.

By 12 May, about 60 *Edinburgh* survivors had arrived aboard the cruiser *Trinidad* as passengers, settling themselves in the canteen recreation space. This had to be shared with an equal number of merchant seamen survivors of various nationalities from bombed and torpedoed ships of earlier convoys. In spite of the cramped quarters they were all happy enough to be returning home, particularly in a heavily armed cruiser which could well defend herself against attack. And those attacks would surely come in the sunlit nights that assisted the enemy but gave no cover to the British ships running the gauntlet between North Norway and the Ice Barrier. Just before midnight on 13 May, *Trinidad* left the Kola inlet in the grey aura of the Arctic night, with the sun low on the horizon peering through a thin veil of mist.

Throughout history, the sailing of a ship on the 13th has been regarded by seamen as an omen of bad luck and this was no exception. Many of the *Trinidad* and *Edinburgh* men openly expressed their apprehension. Two close friends of Jim Harper, a *Trinidad* seaman, confided in him that they did not expect to live much longer. They seemed aware of their fate yet behaved as though all was well to everyone else. Strangely enough, the number 13 had loomed significantly in recent months in respect of the Arctic convoys. The convoy in which *Trinidad* had torpedoed herself and had nearly sunk in March had been PQ13. And the convoy of 13 ships *Edinburgh* had escorted out of the Kola inlet on 28 April had resulted in her sinking. Now *Trinidad* was sailing on the dreaded date, the 13th.

The survivors in the recreation space made themselves as comfortable as circumstances would permit, wishing they could be engaged in some useful occupation rather than sit around doing nothing waiting for the enemy assault which would surely follow in the next few hours. From the bridge the commanding officer, Captain Leslie Saunders, scanned the horizon with binoculars looking for the Russian support planes. The Russians had given a firm assurance that fighter protection would be provided for the first 250 miles of the outward voyage and eventually three planes made a brief appearance but after 20 miles they disappeared over the horizon to return to the Vaenga base. Now 130 miles out, a Condor German reconnaisance plane appeared low on the horizon, well outside the range of accurate gunfire, and began sending homing signals to its bases at Petsamo and Kirkenes giving convoy course and position.

Just before sailing Admiral Bonham-Carter had transferred his flag to *Trinidad*, and now he and Captain Saunders discussed the problems that might arise in the event of attack. It was hoped that the northerly course would bring them into the fog patches often found close to the Arctic ice cap, but these were absent and instead icebergs dotted the northern horizon. At about midday on the 14th the conning tower of a U boat was clearly seen about three miles to the north, positioned between the ship and the ice reef. With the frozen barrier barring the way north course alteration had to be made due west but by now it was clear that every U boat in the vicinity had been alerted.

Fortunately, the voyage was not hampered by the responsibility of convoy ships with their 8 knot progress. Indeed the cruiser had as escorts four destroyers. These were the battle-scarred twins *Foresight* and *Forester*, in company with *Somali* and *Matchless*. The first aid repair to *Trinidad*'s hull only permitted a 20 knot maximum speed, and as the two 'F' destroyers had sustained such severe damage in trying to protect *Edinburgh* two weeks earlier it was a case of the crippled helping the crippled.

Throughout that afternoon the mood of apprehension persisted. The streams of signal forms passing to the admiral and the captain were merely confirmation of what every man knew in his heart. The enemy were assembling their forces to strike. Indeed, dramatic developments were already taking place in North Norway. At the German Luftwaffe bases of Banak and Bardufoss feverish preparations were in hand to launch squadrons of planes in a full scale assault on *Trinidad* and its escorts. Here Major Blodorn, operating the Junkers 88 dive-bombing squadron KG30, and Colonel Ernest Roth, flight commander at Bardufoss conducting operations of the air torpedo group flying HE111s, presented final tactical plans to the eager German pilots. These young men, it was rumoured, were part of a crack squadron brought in from Italy to reinforce the Luftwaffe strength in Norway in a determined attempt to annihilate every Russian convoy trying to break through the strait between North Cape and Bear Island.

By 7 o'clock that evening two more shadowing aircraft arrived. They were recognized as Blohm *und* Voss flying boats which circled backwards and forwards on the rim of the horizon. Almost at once their homing signals were intercepted. On the bridge feverish activity developed as signals were dispatched and received and incoming reports studied and discussed between the admiral and Captain Saunders. An hour later two submarines were sighted, one to the north-west against the white-blue haze of ice and the other dead astern. The vultures were gathering.

To say weather conditions favoured the enemy would be a gross understatement. They could never have been more suitable. Weeks earlier, both *Trinidad* and *Edinburgh* had been able to take refuge in snow squalls and fog banks in their voyages to North Russia. But now there was no fog, no snow flurries, no sea mist, no banks of low lying cloud in which to hide. Instead light fluffy clouds hung high against the blue sky, a perfect screen for the accustomed run-in attack. And of course there would be no darkness.

Then at 9 o'clock that night came the dreaded but expected news. In the radar compartment, bright against a black screen, the searching arm disclosed the approaching enemy with frightening clarity. Formation after formation of aircraft between the bearings 180 and 240 degrees were shown heading at speed in the direction of the cruiser. Reports to the bridge became almost continuous: 'A wave of aircraft at 15 miles', 'Another at 30 miles', 'There are more coming in at 40 miles', 'More at 60 miles'; and then from the radar desk the report which could not have been more complete, more spine-chilling in its finality – 'The screen is full of aircraft, sir'.

Almost at once alarm bells rang with that insistent clamour which only those who have experienced the sound can understand. A nerve shattering cacophony of noise, involuntarily jolting the body into action to set the heart racing and the blood pulsating at critical pressure. 'Action stations – Action. Prepare to repel enemy aircraft.' The brittle metallic voice of the loudspeakers hurled the words into every nook and cranny of the ship. Seconds later, a loud click on the speakers signalled yet another announcement, 'Key personnel not employed at action stations are to disperse throughout the ship'. The order, ominous, foreboding, was meant to ensure that if there were casualties there might still be a nucleus of responsible crew to take charge and act as replacements. In the event it served only to magnify the anxiety created by the first announcement, particularly for the passengers down below with nothing to do but wait and speculate.

Here, in the area of the recreation space, the *Edinburgh* men selected places they considered might give them protection. A corner near the canteen here, a recess by a bulkhead there, or a nook behind a stanchion. They settled down, drew their thick duffel coats more closely round and waited quietly, listening to the drumming of boots along the steel upper deck and the clanging of iron ladders as men raced up and down to their appointed action stations. And then the noise subsided and was replaced by silence, a long silence.

Around the bridge superstructure look-outs searched the skies, peering with aching eyes through heavy binoculars. Attired in anti-flash gear of white hoods and long white gloves, men at the guns stood tense, motionless, fingers nervously feeling for curved triggers, waiting in silence, each alone with his own thoughts. There were few whose lips did not move almost imperceptibly, committing themselves to God's keeping. Even those who in the past had vehemently denied His existence found comfort in mute supplication.

It would soon be midnight but the cover of darkness into which they might have escaped would not be there. Instead the orange tinted sun hung poised on the rim of the horizon along the southern sky.

Then came the first low whisper of the enemy. The author, standing on the bridge beside Captain Saunders and Admiral Bonham-Carter heard the pulsating hum, growing louder with every passing second. There was no further need for radar reports for the first wave of bombers were already in sight. Small black dots against the ceiling of the Arctic world, they began a game of hide-and-seek, darting from the cover of one thin cloud to another. On the ship every eye peered anxiously into the scattered haze, while at the guns fingers closed more tightly around trigger keys. Darting out of the sky in concerted movement, the bombers peeled off and came screaming down at near vertical angles, their engines racing.

But even as they began their dives the cruiser's guns blasted a defensive curtain of fire. A deafening roar that set the senses reeling as the barrage from the combined power of the 4-inch anti-aircraft guns, 2 pounders, pom-poms and oerlikons went into action. With it, barely audible in the thunder of battle, came the voice of the first lieutenant, Lieut-Commander Jack Herrapath, air defence officer, over the loud speaker system directing gun crews on to targets from his observation position half-way up the mast. With startling clarity, the first of the bombs were falling. Small and dark at first against the sky, they tumbled from the belly of the planes in a whining, wobbling descent of flight. Suddenly they were falling around the ship, missing by 40, 50 or 100 feet astern and abeam. Exploding on contact with the sea in ear-splitting eruptions, great waterspouts cascaded high above the ship's funnels, hanging momentarily before falling in an ice-cold deluge on the gunners in open cock-pits round the superstructure.

The ship lurched and shook under the impact and the hastily welded plates over the great wound in the hull strained at the joints, creaking in protest. Below decks, the concussion was frightening – an empty tank belaboured by sledge hammers. But this was only the first of many, for now the sky became a procession of aircraft waiting to attack. Plane after plane came storming down out of the clouds, releasing its bombs and levelling out at only 400 feet above mast height, engines accelerating to a shattering climax.

It became a battle of wits between *Trinidad*'s captain and the aircraft pilots. As each plane began its power drive, it meant for Captain Saunders the responsibility of making a split second decision, to the left or to the right, anticipating the fall of each stick of bombs. At such limited speed there was little room for manoeuvre and errors of judgement were unthinkable. In the moment the bombs left the planes lay the decision between life and death. Down the tube to the wheel-house below came the captain's voice, crisp, decisive, competent, 'Hard to port'. A voice betraying neither anxiety nor dismay. If he were right the bombs would miss but if he were wrong. ... slowly, agonisingly slowly, in an intermission of nail-biting deadness of movement the ship began to swing away from the line of falling bombs. Again the swing was enough but only just enough and the bombs plunged into the sea only yards away. Destroyer crews watched as the cruiser was obscured by a wall of exploding water and then emerged undamaged. But they *were* right decisions. Although the accompanying destroyers were receiving their share of the dive-bombing the main concentration was upon *Trinidad*. Below in her recreation space the *Edinburgh* men crouched and waited, listening to the nightmare of explosions against the hull, wondering if the next bomb would be the one to come inboard. Within the crowded area there were many Indian seamen and they began to pray aloud to their gods – to Allah, to Vishnu and to Shiva – for protection. The babble of voices grew louder as the minutes passed and the danger became more imminent.

Again and again, the Stukas and Junkers came snarling down, sometimes singly, sometimes in groups of two or three. Uppermost in the mind of Captain Saunders and the admiral must have been the thought, 'Even if we avoid a direct hit, just how long can the welded plates take the battering from the near misses?' Each explosion, followed by showers of shrapnel, sent a mighty shudder along the damaged hull but still the plates held. Unceasingly the guns of the cruiser blasted their high explosive shells into the paths of the oncoming bombers. For nearly two hours the attacks continued as formations of aircraft replaced those returning to base. But while the gunners were fully occupied in fighting off the planes overhead, a new emergency arose. Over the speakers came the clear call, 'Stand by to repel torpedo bombers bearing red 90'. Racing in from the south they appeared low on the horizon, a line of eight, wing-tip to wing-tip. As they neared, the shape and size of Heinkel 115s and 111s, each carrying two torpedoes, became more clearly defined. They came in low skimming just above the water, line ahead in a wide circle. Sections of the already exhausted gun crews were immediately diverted to the new targets, depressing the guns until they were firing downwards at the oncoming planes, while the greater part of the armament concentrated on the Junkers and Stukas above.

If the line of Heinkels was allowed to reach the dropping zone there would be little chance of avoiding a wide span of a possible 16 torpedoes, streaking through the water at 40 knots. But by now the destroyers had seen the new assault and suddenly the formation was broken by the intensity of the barrage. The line began to swerve and the foremost planes lurched and weaved in a desperate effort to avoid destruction. Skidding and rolling from side to side they turned from the shells bursting among them. Sweeping around in a huge circle, they were back minutes later in two formations of line abreast. This time they approached from different directions, on the quarter and abeam. But once more the fire power from *Trinidad* and the destroyers proved too devastating and again they turned away. Then, as if the odds against were not enough, look-outs suddenly reported at least 4 U boats surfaced to the north and east. Twice repulsed, the Heinkels came again, two formations now, one on the port and the other on the starboard quarter. Weaving from side to side to avoid destruction, they pressed home their assault. Simultaneously, each loosed the first of their two torpedoes at near surface level. Fortunately the silver tracks could be clearly seen against the grey black water and the helm was swiftly swung to starboard, then to midships. In this way the captain presented the cruiser's stern, the minimum target, to the trails and seconds later the torpedoes sped by on either side.

Meanwhile, the Stukas and Junkers pressed home their attacks in a cleverly planned co-operated movement with the Heinkels and the torpedo bombers, gathering for the kill, came in again in one massed group on the port beam. Despite the barrage of fire they reached the dropping zone and simultaneously launched their torpedoes. At the same time a single Junkers, roaring out of the thin cloud immediately overhead, released its stick of four bombs. In a desperate bid to present the minimum target the bows of *Trinidad* swung into the narrow lanes of the torpedoes. At once over the speakers came the urgent and anguished cry of the air defence officer, 'Starboard pom-poms, starboard pom-poms'. But it was already too late. The cruiser in the middle of the turn, swinging wildly to port in an effort to avoid the torpedoes, was moving directly into the line of the falling bombs. Alternatives no longer existed. It was bombs or torpedoes; the outcome inevitable. Despite the helm hard over and the ship shuddering under her maximum speed, there was no escape.

Personnel on the bridge watched with bated breath as the wobbling, screaming 500lb bombs fell directly towards the superstructure. With them came the roar of the Junkers' engines pulling out from its dive barely above mast height and the thunder and clamour of the ship's guns blasting a stream of shells into the attacking aircraft. Reduced to a fireball the German plane plunged into the sea away on the port beam.

The impact of four 500lb bombs exploding almost simultaneously was terrifying. The little world around the bridge superstructure disintegrated into a pocket earthquake, blinding the senses, sending the bridge deck leaping. Officers and ratings were hurled in all directions. The damage to the ship was catastrophic. Each of the bombs had been on target. One had fallen outboard, gliding along the side of the ship aft of the foreward 'B' turret, in line with the bridge. Here it exploded under the waterline, blowing off the temporarily welded plates and sending a wall of water into the magazine and cordite compartments below the turret. All were instantly flooded, drowning every rating battened down in the area. If the explosion had occurred above the waterline flame and not water would have reached the cordite, in which case the ship and every man aboard would have disappeared in one great ball of fire.

The patched-up bulkheads were torn apart like paper and with tons of water pouring in through the 60 ft hole, the ship took an immediate list to starboard. Two other bombs grazed the port side, outboard, exploding abreast the foc's'le and puncturing the forward compartments causing immediate flooding. But the greatest damage was caused by the fourth bomb which landed a few feet in front of the bridge. The armour piercing head smashed its way through the admiral's sea cabin, the Fleet Air Arm office, and exploded in the area of the canteen recreation space and the stokers' and petty officers' mess decks. It reduced these compartments into a devil's scrapyard. Here the great energy of the explosion, magnified by the confines of the area, was directed forwards and upwards. The blast smashed its way up through the foc's'le deck to form a great crater some 40 feet by 20 feet between the bridge and 'B' turret. The bridge compass platform had miraculously escaped the worst of the damage but even so the admiral and one or two officers were flung dazed into the sides of the bridge structure while the captain was hurled on to the bridge screen.

The crater itself had now developed into a cauldron of fire, with flames creeping rapidly aft under the superstructure. Other factors arose from the damage contributing to the gravity of the situation. The forward fire-main, essential for fire-fighting in the area, was completely destroyed. Forward telephone communication systems had failed and the revolution telegraph system to the engine room was jammed. Despite heroic efforts by damage control parties to extinguish the fires there was little they could do without pressure of water and the flames spread rapidly. The captain was faced with a critical decision. More torpedo bombers had arrived and were deploying to make another attack. If he stopped the cruiser to fight the fires the ship would be an easy target for the enemy planes but if he maintained speed to dodge the torpedoes the fires could well reach unmanageable proportions. He took the latter course. There was always the possibility that the fires could be mastered but there was little chance of the ship surviving a torpedo hit.

The carnage in the area of the recreation space where the passenger survivors had taken refuge defied description. The explosion had torn away steel bulkheads like cardboard. Decking between the recreation space and the messdecks around and below had been ripped apart with a giant hand; stanchions, handrails and piping were twisted like wire into grotesque shapes. Few in this area survived the holocaust.

It seemed that the tragedies and misfortunes which had

beset the men of *Edinburgh* since the start of their voyage from Iceland early in April still pursued them. This first group of survivors to be returned to the United Kingdom had been overwhelmed by a disaster of the first magnitude. The apprehension survivors had felt back in the Russian camps for the return voyage had not been misplaced.

Assistant canteen manager Jack Holman had a miraculous escape and takes up the story from here.

When the bomb exploded in the next compartment there was a massive yellow flash. I was hurled forward, hitting the bulkhead and losing consciousness. When I recovered, blood was pouring from a gash on my forehead and a split under the eye. In fact my eyes were so filled with blood, I thought at first I was blind. The ship was listing over at such an angle that I had to crawl downwards towards the ship's side and from there I stumbled along, blindly feeling my way, climbing over and through the twisted girders and bulkheads which had been torn from the decking. My physical condition was bad enough but the situation was aggravated by the darkness and the volume of smoke pouring up from below, enveloping me like a blanket. How I found the ladder leading to the upper deck, I'll never know. Coughing and gasping for breath I managed to make it to the top, feeling the cold fresh air on my face. Suddenly, strong arms were reaching down and pulling me upwards and outwards on to the deck. I must have been the last man out from the area below, the last of only eight, for the recreation space in which the *Edinburgh* men and the merchant seamen had been accommodated had been utterly destroyed.

In this same area, a damage control party which had been assembled at action stations was completely wiped out. Just before the bombs fell eight of the radar operators, who were free of duty now that the transmitting station was out of action, were on the flag deck watching the bombs fall, frequently taking cover from shrapnel. They were well aware it was only a matter of time before hits would be scored. Three of them asked the senior radar operator Jack Anderson if they should stay on top or find a safer refuge in one of the compartments below. His opinion was that they should stay where they were and they agreed, remarking that as they had come through the earlier action together in March, if they had to go they might as well go together. The others, including Able Seaman Jim Harper, a radar operator, decided it would be safer below. But as they neared the recreation space the bombs exploded immediately ahead. Harper relates.

I lay on the deck, at the foot of the ladder leading to the Captain's sea-going cabin and the bridge. I heard the first bomb go off somewhere nearby and a moment later, another seemed to explode about twenty feet away, throwing a lot of debris over my head. I was aware of something tearing down through the bridge structure, like a machine crashing through plywood. I covered my face with my arms, as a grey shape shot through the deck in front of me. I saw it between my arms. A blinding sheet of flame enveloping me as the iron rivets burst from the deck on which I lay. I was aware of being lifted into the air, with the deck curling around me like paper. Later I came to – how much later I don't know. It seemed very quiet, then high above me there was a tinkle of a small piece of metal falling. Suddenly I realized the air was hot, in fact the deck and bulkheads which my groping hands touched were growing hotter every minute. Through the dense billowing smoke pouring out from somewhere just ahead, I noticed the dull glow of fire. With my senses clearing rapidly, I realized I had to get out quickly. I remember stepping through a hole in the bulkhead and eventually finding myself in the hangar space and staggering out on to the catapult deck, to feel the ice cold air hitting me in the face. I was pretty shaken up but still alive and in one piece. I learned later that my three mess-mates who had come below with me, were blown to pieces. Two of them being my close friends whose earlier premonition had proved sadly and tragically correct.

Damage control and rescue parties, arriving on 'B' gun deck, found the area a complete shambles. The gun turret itself had been pushed over at a crazy angle and in addition to the huge crater in the deck part of the ship's side had been blown away. From below, there were cries for help and they hurriedly lowered ropes. Five men were eventually hauled out: one an asdic rating who ran around in circles, vomiting all the time. The limit of the explosion damage reached down as far as No 1 transmitter room. It was here young ordinary seaman William Cutler found himself as he slowly recovered consciousness, covered in blood from the bodies of two other seamen lying on top of him.

Just forward of 'B' gun deck, 'A' turret and its crew had fortunately escaped the worst of the blast. The cumulative effect of the shock waves from the bombs had distorted the ship enough to jam escape hatches. A description of this was given by wardroom steward Howard Stephens, whose action station was in the magazine of 'A' turret deep down in the ship.

In these compartments, well below the waterline, any noise in the sea around is greatly amplified by the water. The explosion of the bombs from the near misses along the side of the ship was indeed terrifying. Suddenly there was one great explosion and I was knocked unconscious. When I recovered, I found I was lying under a pile of cordite cases, for the heavy timbers supporting the racks had snapped. I climbed the ladder and tried to get out, but found the hatch had jammed. I don't think I shall ever forget the dread and dismay that came over me in those awful moments, when I realized that I was trapped in this steel cell and within a ship which was probably sinking. Trying to control the panic which I felt building up inside me, I tore at the dogs and catches of the hatch but they were immovable. I recall picking up a small iron bar and banging violently on the metal roof and then shouting until my throat could take no more.

I could hear the shells rolling about on the deck in the shell room above me and had practically given up hope, when I heard footsteps – someone was up there. The reborn hope gave me new energy to wield my bar and shout. Suddenly there was an answering call, some banging at the hatch and the catches began to turn. Within minutes, the cover was back and I was out and free. However, as we were talking, the increasing list of the ship brought down a whole rack of six-inch shells from one bulkhead, barely missing us. But by now the hatch out of the shell room had also become jammed. There was however, a possible way of escape through a small opening in which the shell hoist operated. Shirts off, we squeezed our sweating bodies through the tiny opening and we were free. The deck on the port side was a blazing inferno, with spouting burning debris erupting from a large crater in the deck, like a firework display.

Jack Cook, a coder, felt that the Fleet Air Arm office would probably be about the safest place in the ship but one of the four bombs came crashing through within a few feet of him. It ploughed on down to the decks below and exploded in one violent upheaval. Relating his experience, Cook said.

I was suddenly lifted and then seemed to be propelled swiftly into another world, although still held by this one. I seemed to be floating and the image of my wife and little girl floated with me within a feeling of utter tranquillity. I felt for my body but it wasn't there – I couldn't see and I couldn't hear but I could think. After a while, there was a whirling sensation and with a rush I came back to this world to find myself pinned down with debris and with four others around me calling for help.

Soon willing hands were pulling at the heavy equipment on top of us and carrying us out on to another deck. With others, I was placed by the rail to be taken off in the first rescuing destroyer to come alongside. I was quite blind and paralysed all over; the top of my head had been opened, my right eye damaged and my fingers broken. I felt quite a mess. I think at this moment the realization of my condition brought a sense of revelation, when I was aware that material things were of no avail whatsoever, but there was a spirit which would survive in some form or another.

Inside 'B' turret itself, the force of the explosion had been so great that bits and pieces of equipment flew in all directions. Captain Richard Griffiths, Royal Marines, who was in charge of this turret ordered one of his marines to shout down to the magazine crews and tell them to come up at once. There was no reply and when he and Sergeant John Feltham listened at the hatch all they could hear was water cascading into the compartments. In the shell room directly above these spaces the water was coming in so rapidly that it was waist high before the last few men could escape.

Able seaman Arthur Wilbourne and some others, who had found themselves trapped in one of the compartments under the bridge, managed to fight their way through to the inside of the hangar. When they arrived instead of a way of escape they found the Walrus flying boat – used for U boat reconnaisance – in flames. In the confined space and darkness of the hangar the fumes and heat became overpowering. The observer, Sub-Lieutenant Paul House made an attempt to turn a hose on the burning plane but as most of the fire-main was out of action all he got was a dribble of water from the nozzle. In a matter of minutes the situation was out of control. The prime consideration now became escape. The only way out was through the heavy hangar doors but first they had to be opened by raising them from the bottom with chains. Bomb blast had buckled the doors like everything else and pull as they might they could only raise them about 12 inches. Fortunately this was enough and one by one all of them, including the pilot Lieutenant 'Jock' Thomson, managed to slide underneath to comparative safety.

All the while, the damage control parties were doing their utmost to put out the fires and restrict the flooding. To counteract the increasing list to starboard it became necessary to counterflood by letting even more water into the ship on the port side. This operation had a beneficial if temporary effect as it prevented the ship listing even further and perhaps capsizing but she was now deeper in the water. Even where the fire parties could get at the seat of the fire their efforts were hampered by choking black smoke from burning oil fuel. Although valiant efforts were made in many areas the intensity of the heat and smoke and the lack of water pressure made the task impossible.

The engineer constructor Lieutenant Michael Chatter, with the assistance of stoker petty officer Jack Shepherd, managed to penetrate as far forward as the engine room artificers' mess where they could hear men trapped below shouting for help. They attached a hose to the fire main but finding there was no pressure they sent for protective clothing. This arrived quickly and after putting it on they tried once more to penetrate the smoke. The heat, however, was far too great and they had to abandon the attempt.

The fire raging in the hangar had by now heated the deck above to such an extent that the ready-use ammunition was igniting. Pom-pom and machine gun rounds started exploding in all directions, producing a lethal firework display.

Although *Trinidad* had been mortally hit she was still

fighting on. No quarter is given to a sinking ship and the torpedo bombers were again gathering to attack. Twice more the helm was ordered hard over to present the minimum target of the stern towards the torpedo tracks which then raced harmlessly by. Five minutes later three pairs of torpedo bombers came in low, skimming the surface, to release their torpedoes at the port side. Once again the bright pointers of the tracer shells from the smaller guns gave excellent direction to the 4-inch guns. Though the Heinkels succeeded in dropping their deadly tin fish their concentrated attack was so broken up by this barrage that none found its mark.

Down below, the timber shores and oil fuel leakages were rapidly igniting and adding to the conflagration already established. By 11.50 p.m. the enemy attacks began to ease off and at last Captain Saunders was able to lessen the fanning of the flames by reducing speed to 12 knots but by now this was too late to do much good. At midnight, with the sun lifting clear above the horizon, the fires were completely out of control. Below there were still those who remained alive, dazed and wounded, trying to grope their way past flames and through choking smoke to safety. Below them again, compartments had become sealed off by fire trapping the men in them at their duty stations. The bridge itself was becoming untenable as the superstructure became a chimney for the fire below. The flames roared up the bridge companion ways and out through the ladder openings.

The state of the ship was so grave, with U boats in the vicinity and further attacks inevitable, that the captain decided to abandon ship. The engines were stopped and he broadcast throughout the vessel, instructing everyone to muster on the quarter-deck in their respective divisions and warning them not to go back to any part to collect personal belongings. On the emergency bridge, the admiral and the captain summoned Commander Hugh Skinner, the constructor. He arrived some minutes later breathless and blackened with smoke. The admiral asked him, 'Skinner, we have ordered abandon ship. Were we right?' To which he replied, 'Sir, it would take the whole Glasgow fire brigade to put out that fire'.

When the order to abandon came through to 'B' turret, it was discovered that the force of the bomb blasts had jammed the main exit door. The gun crew had to scramble out one by one along the gun barrels to drop on what was left of the gun deck. Deep down in the bowels of the ship in the telephone exchange below the stokers' messdeck, able seaman Colin Nicholls, recovering consciousness from the blasts, found himself alone in the darkness. The deck above him had been blown away and the escape ladder with it and on hands and knees he discovered that his two companions had been killed by the explosion. No one seemed to hear his shouts. With stoic resignation, he sat down and lit a cigarette. It was this act that saved his life for at that very moment a stoker was running through a compartment two decks above. He happened to look down as he passed and saw the flare of the match. Soon ropes were lowered and Nicholls was pulled to safety.

Most of the survivors had by now assembled on the quarterdeck, waiting in orderly divisions for the destroyers to come to take them off. The destroyer *Matchless* was the first to arrive. She nosed carefully in aft of amidships, with great skill and due regard for the flames roaring around the bridge and the exploding ammunition. All the stretcher cases were loaded on to her decks, followed by many wounded men who were able to get aboard with assistance from willing hands. The transfer was completed courageously and successfully. The other three destroyers circled round continuously providing a screen to keep the U boats at bay. Here and there in the sky there were still white wisps of smoke like cotton wool and occasional columns of water, the results of anti-aircraft shell bursts and exploding bombs, suddenly appeared before falling back into the sea.

Despite the gravity of the situation, there were lighter moments. In the middle of a highly tense and dramatic episode a man appeared in a sorry condition. He seemed to be blind and not to know what was happening to him. With compassion and great difficulty, despite his protests, they eventually managed to lift, push and pull him over the side on to the deck of the destroyer. It was then they discovered he hadn't been wounded at all. The man, extremely short-sighted, had simply lost his glasses. Radio mechanic John Evans, dressed only in shirt and trousers, was climbing over the rails on to the last destroyer to come alongside when another rating came along *Trinidad*'s deck. Although the ship was burning fiercely and sinking slowly under him the man found time to shout across, 'Can I interest you in a new line of gent's natty overcoats?', and threw one over to Evans.

One personality that stood out through this catastrophe was the master-at-arms, Clifford Avent. He positioned himself on the top of the after capstan and used a hand megaphone to muster the men into four groups so that each destroyer would receive an equal allocation.

A little earlier shipwright Bert Soper had decided to go below to collect another coat. On the way he passed his friend 'Blackie' Cass lying down in one of the gangways wrapped in a duffel coat. He said, 'What the hell are you doing down here?', to which Cass replied, 'I decided to try to get some sleep.' Soper hauled him to his feet with, 'What! Go to sleep with the bloody ship sinking. Get up top.' Passing through the fire area on the way to the upper deck they were transfixed by the sight of a seaman trapped in a light steel bulkhead which had been wrapped tightly round him by the force of the explosion. As the flames roared nearer he was screaming his way to death. Every fire main in the area was out of action and nothing could be done to extricate him.

It was at this time that a very gallant rescue attempt was made by engineer lieutenant John Boddy. Some of his stokers were trapped below and could be heard shouting for help. The tall, very young, faired-haired officer stepped through a hatchway to the decks below with the remark, 'Can't leave my men below – must try to get them out.' That part of the ship was by now a raging inferno. There was no ladder and the rope he used to lower himself must have broken or burnt through. Although a search party was organized it was driven back by the intense heat. Lieutenant Boddy and the men he had tried to rescue had perished. He had been married just a week or two before the ship left Devonport. Now he had sacrificed his life to reach his men. Later in the war he was posthumously awarded the Albert Medal – subsequently renamed the George Cross.

In quick succession, the two 'F' destroyers pulled in alongside the quarterdeck and in orderly groups the *Trinidad* men jumped or scrambled over the guardrails. There were sighs of relief from the survivors aboard the two destroyers as they drew away for by this time the flames were so close to 'A' turret magazine that it only needed a chance spark to blow the whole lot sky high. It was also a relief to see that although there were a few enemy torpedo and reconnaisance planes circling around the Germans had stopped attacking for the time being.

Petty officer Harold Sowden was one of the last to arrive on the quarterdeck. The gunnery officer Lieut-Commander Frederick Larken saw he was carrying a torch so summoned him to accompany the first lieutenant, Lieut-Commander Jack Herapath, in a final search. They went below and searched every compartment it was humanly possible to reach and checked that no injured were left behind. By the time they reached the upper deck again the last of the rescuing destroyers *Somali* was drawing alongside. It was at this moment that one of the remaining torpedo bombers chose to come in on the port quarter, in a determined effort to apply the *coup de grâce*. High up on the 4-inch gun-deck commissioned gunner Dicky Bunt and gunner Charles Norsworthy were manning the guns to the last to cover the remaining survivors while they climbed aboard the destroyer. Dicky Bunt, running between the port and starboard sides of the gun deck, was the first to spot the oncoming plane. With a shout of 'Nosser, there's one bastard coming in over there', they jumped on to the port gun mounting and watched the aircraft through binoculars and telescopic sights. The plane, approaching fast, was only about twenty feet above the sea and a mile away when first spotted. All the electrical circuits used to train and elevate the gun had been destroyed so the two men were reduced to the primitive method of controlling the mounting by hand. With both barrels loaded they waited. With the cruiser listing to starboard they had an additional difficulty when they tried to depress the sights sufficiently to pick up the target. Norsworthy applied his eye to the telescope and directed the gun as best he could. Dicky Bunt, peering through the binoculars, shouted, 'train left – train left – stop – up a bit – train right', and so on. Changing to look through the open cartwheel sight Norsworthy lowered the guns a little, to give him a target sighting between the bottom of the plane and the sea, and then fired both barrels. It was a masterful effort for both shells burst about three feet under the plane's port wing, lifting it with such a jerk that it almost capsized. A great cheer went up from the men who watched. The enemy's torpedo dropped off at a crazy angle while smoke and flame poured out of the fuselage. Turning sharply away, the Heinkel slowly lost height and disappeared into the sea. These were the last shells to be fired from *Trinidad*.

The two gunners were the men of the moment. But for their initiative and skill in preventing this attack the casualties would have been much higher as it is not likely that the unharrassed torpedo bomber would have missed the stationary cruiser. Dicky Bunt lost his life later in the war, in an action in the Indian Ocean.

As the ship increased its list to starboard, the two gunners joined the last few survivors who were having difficulty in finding a footing on the sloping decks. Several men were acting as anchor men by attaching themselves to the higher guardrail. From each of these a dozen or more men hung, clinging together in a human chain, and this prevented men tumbling into the lower scuppers which were now awash. Lying on deck at the extremity of these chains was Commander George Collet. He was directing each man in turn to let go and slide down to the lower rail, before climbing up *Somali*'s side. Able seamen Charles Ideson and Jim Harper were among the last to make this difficult and awkward climb. They were amused by the spectacle of the captain's steward jumping for the destroyer, with one hand tightly clutching the captain's gold braided uniform neatly arranged on its hangar. As Ideson's and Harper's feet touched the deck they turned to help those following. Their hands reached down to haul up a rather short chubby man dressed in a black jersey who was a stranger to them, followed by the commander. A moment or two later willing hands were helping up the last man to leave the ship, Captain Saunders.

The four destroyers stood off for some minutes to watch the last moments of the cruiser. The canting deck and settling bows revealed the distressed condition of the stricken ship. Profiled against a background of rolling clouds of black smoke, red tongues of flame from the forward turrets to the catapult deck ravaged the bridge and superstructure. The fire had reached the after boiler room for now great clouds of smoke issued from the after funnel. To hasten her end Admiral Bonham-Carter on *Somali* gave the unpleasant but obvious order to *Matchless* to sink

Trinidad with torpedoes. Aboard this destroyer, the crew and survivors watched the tubes being trained on the burning ship. When the levers went over the torpedoes streaked through the water towards the target. Everyone aboard stood gazing out across the grey stretch of sea between the two ships. In a few seconds the warheads were there, embedding themselves into the starboard side of the hull below the bridge. The muffled explosions of the death blows echoed across the water as the ship, shuddering under their impact, buried her bows in the icy sea. A third torpedo, punching into the same target area, must have almost cut her in two because three or four minutes later *Trinidad* slowly moved forward and downward. From the main and after masts the large battle ensigns flaunted their emblems as if in defiance of the enemy and the leaping flames below them. From a signal halyard on the main mast a short line of flags, already scorched by the heat, fluttered in the breeze broadcasting her last message to the world, 'I am sailing to the westward'.

From the decks of the destroyers the survivors watched, realizing that within the sinking hull a great number of their messmates were being committed to the deep, and that a number of *Edinburgh* men who had embarked with such high hopes of returning home to be re-united with their wives and families were now dead, entombed within the disappearing ship. As the water reached the bridge, the stern lifted itself clear of the water. There she seemed to hang suspended for a few seconds as if reluctant to die. Then with a rush she plunged forward to disappear in an upsurging cloud of smoke and steam. It was twenty-past one; the date 15 May – Ascension Day.

Into the construction of the *Trinidad* had gone all that was best of modern technical equipment. The loss of this brand new cruiser was a heavy blow to the British Home Fleet. The ship, with the men, weapons and machinery, had been integrated into a highly sophisticated unit, tested and proved in action. In minutes, only a widening circle of bubbling water marked her grave. A fleeting and tragic memorial to a gallant cruiser. So *Trinidad* sank to the bed of the Barents Sea – on the same ocean floor as HMS *Edinburgh*, no great distance away. There she would lie, joining the many cargo vessels which had fallen victim to enemy submarines and aircraft.

As the destroyers sped away at 22 knots to the westward, Harper and Ideson were sitting on the quarter-deck, thankfully drinking the hot tea which *Somali*'s crew had brewed up. The short chubby stranger whom they had hauled aboard from *Trinidad* came over and said, 'May I be allowed to sit with you chaps?' They immediately made room for him and when he was as comfortable as conditions would permit he turned to them with a smile and said, 'You lads probably don't know me and I hope you won't throw me overboard when I tell you who I am. You see, I'm rather a Jonah, *Trinidad* is the fifth ship that has gone under me – I'm Admiral Bonham-Carter.' He talked away for some time, until a *Somali* officer came along and asked him if he was the admiral. He left them with, 'Sorry I have to leave you, but this is where I have to put the gold braid on again.'

By now the four destroyers, crammed with survivors, were putting as much distance as possible between them and the German airfields, increasingly aware of the German reconnaisance planes which never left but shadowed them continuously. The speed of both *Foresight* and *Forester* was still limited by the boiler damage inflicted in their gallant defence of the *Edinburgh*. Of the four destroyers, *Somali* was to be torpedoed in those same waters by a U boat in four months' time with the loss of some 40 men, and in three months Italian aircraft in the Mediterranean were to sink *Foresight*. Only *Matchless* and *Forester* survived the bitter war.

Within an hour another wave of Junkers approached and subjected the destroyers to further bombing attacks. Again the misses were uncomfortably near and survivors on the decks of *Foresight* were kept busy playing a dramatic hide-and-seek exercise on either side of the funnel and superstructure, keeping it between them and the flying shrapnel. One of the few surviving Lascars from the bombed recreation space brought out his prayer mat and placed it pointing in the direction of Mecca before prostrating himself to give thanks to Allah for his continued existence. Below decks the gangways were crowded with injured men lying around. Mess tables were being used for the more badly wounded who had to receive medical attention where they lay.

The admiral decided that the small force should seek the protection of the fleet as soon as possible. To this end he instructed a signal to be sent to Scapa Flow, asking the commander-in-chief for help from his covering forces. Unfortunately they were unable to contact any shore station, partly due to the great distance involved but mainly because atmospheric conditions close to the Norwegian coast were particularly difficult. Instead a standard broadcast was made to all ships in the hope it would be picked up by one of them. As time passed, a signal was intercepted indicating that German cruisers with a destroyer escort might have set out from Norway with the clear intention of cutting off their retreat. Later signals reported unidentified ships approaching from the south and that sighting could be expected in about one hour. Aware that the enemy warships *Tirpitz*, *Admiral Scheer*, *Hipper* and *Prinz Eugen* could easily sally out from their bases in Norway, the distant horizon was anxiously scanned. The crews of each destroyer closed up at action stations, loaded their guns and stood ready. Sure enough, within the hour eight or nine small specks appeared on the southern rim of the sea.

It seemed to the watching crews and survivors that here was yet another misfortune and one that could only have a fatal ending. No one dared to express such a morbid thought because in every sense they were all in the same boat. Instead there was a general impression of calm acceptance of the inevitable. Yet the watchers were to witness one more example of the tenacity and defiance called for by the traditions of the Royal Navy.

Signals between the four ships were rapidly exchanged and suddenly with a little increased speed *Foresight, Forester* and *Matchless* made a tight turn towards the north away from the approaching ships. *Somali*, the only one of the four destroyers left with a full quota of torpedoes, was to sweep to the south to meet the oncoming forces. The plan was evident. If these were the German ships, she would intercept and engage them in a delaying action which might provide a little time for the three other destroyers to make good their escape to the west. It would be a sacrificial attempt, which against the superior fire power of so many ships would amount to suicide. Here was one little destroyer, crammed with survivors, facing up to what looked to be a considerable German fleet with only four 4.7-inch guns with which to do battle. It was another reminder of Sir Richard Grenville's action off the Azores against the great Spanish galleons, when 'the little Revenge ran on and on'.

Then from the distant ships little pin pricks of light flashed repeatedly. Were these the first of the gun flashes that could be expected? But in the following moments a great cheer went up from everyone. It could now be seen that the flickers of light were from signalling lamps identifying themselves as units of the British 10th Cruiser Squadron. To the watchers it seemed almost unbelievable at first but as the vessels neared there was no mistaking the shapes of the great cruisers. Here were *Kent, Norfolk* and *Liverpool*, followed by *Nigeria* flying the flag of Rear-Admiral Harold Burroughs. These ships were escorted by destroyers and had arrived to shepherd the group back to Iceland. The welcome squadron had placed itself between the menacing enemy and the destroyers. It was a timely arrival.

Within twenty minutes the ships had joined to form a wide arrow head with the four cruisers in the van and the destroyer *Foresight* on the tip of the port wing. Hardly had this formation taken shape when the asdic detected a submerged submarine not far astern. Immediately *Foresight* made a turn to the south and commenced her run in for the attack. When over the area she dropped a pattern of depth charges and made another turn to port. With the echoes becoming louder and faster the second pattern exploded, but with the cruiser squadron moving further and further away it was no time to hang about hunting U boats. *Foresight* broke off the action, increased speed to the limited maximum of 27 knots and rejoined them but not before a look-out had reported seeing the bow of a U boat rise above the surface and slowly sink back. Confirmation of a kill was never established.

Inside an hour the air was filled with the sound of attacking aircraft, diving out of the lowering clouds. The concentration of anti-aircraft fire from the British ships was extremely heavy yet the German pilots still pressed home their attacks. Roaring down through the blanket of flak in almost vertical dives dropping their bombs as they levelled off, they managed to climb out of danger. Walls of water thrown up by near misses would at times completely hide one or other of the cruisers which were bearing the brunt of the bombing. The Germans developed attack after attack but after five hours, as the distance from the enemy airfields increased, they became less frequent and despite the ferocity of their assault every ship survived the blitzing and came through unscathed.

CHAPTER 11

The German Armed Merchant Ship

WITHIN THE GERMAN NAVAL HIGH COMMAND, the reported destruction of HMS *Trinidad* produced an atmosphere of jubilation, especially following so closely upon the sinking of HMS *Edinburgh* only thirteen days earlier. They were prepared to admit the loss of their two destroyers *Z26* and the *Hermann Schoemann* but against the loss of two of Britain's latest cruisers the scales came down heavily on the side of the Germans. It strengthened the argument Grand-Admiral Raeder had always maintained, that air strength in North Norway was the best method of preventing convoys getting through to North Russia. His frequent appeals to Hitler to direct the commander-in-chief of the German Air Force, Reichsmarschall Hermann Goering, to increase the number of aircraft under Air Command – Norway, had eventually proved successful. Considerable reinforcements were sent to Norway, and the command known as 'Luftflotte V' formed. These included Junkers 88 long range bombers, Heinkel 111s and 115 torpedo bombers, Stuka dive-bombers and long range reconnaisance aircraft including Focke Wolfe Condors. The last, the giant multi-engined Condors, were the key to the situation for they were able to fly long sweeps out into the Arctic Ocean to find the convoys and guide the bomber squadrons in to mount their attack.

The success had prompted some over-optimistic speculation that the British would think twice before sending further convoys through to Murmansk. It was an opinion entirely misplaced and certainly not entertained by the Allies. In Britain, the loss of two such valuable cruisers was a matter of deep concern to the commander-in-chief, Admiral Sir John Tovey, and after discussing the matter with Rear-Admiral Bonham-Carter he supported the latter's recommendation that until aerodromes in North Norway had been neutralized convoys should be postponed until darkness could afford protection. His communication to the Admiralty was explicit, 'If the convoys have to continue for political reasons, then serious and heavy losses must be anticipated'. The First Sea Lord, Admiral of the Fleet Sir Dudley Pound agreed with the judgement. So far as the navy was concerned, they were against the movement of convoys in the Arctic Ocean until the winter darkness set in.

However, in the political arena a different opinion was emerging. In October 1941, Lord Beaverbrook and Mr Averell Harriman had signed an agreement with the Russians in Moscow that specified quantities of supplies would be delivered through the Arctic route by June 1942. Despite British losses, the Russians demanded that the agreement should be honoured. The Americans had in fact made available all the goods and the ships to carry them to meet the promised date. In Iceland and the United Kingdom there were now 106 ships waiting to be escorted to North Russian ports, a fact which President Roosevelt was careful to point out. For Mr Churchill it was a time for momentous decisions. In view of British losses he had to explain to the President the impossibility of speeding up the number of convoys in order to reduce the accumulation of freight ships. Escorts could not be transferred from the Atlantic route to leave Britain's life-blood supply line unprotected. He urged the President not to press him beyond his judgement in the matter until a solution had been found. But only two days later the pressure was increased by a request from Stalin that every possible effort should be made to ensure the safe arrival of the convoy ships now waiting in Iceland as supplies were urgently needed for the Russian front. In reply, Mr Churchill pledged that the Royal Navy would fight their way through the Barents Sea with the maximum amount of war supplies. Later at a meeting of the Chiefs-of-Staffs Committee, he summed up the problem as follows.

> Not only Premier Stalin but President Roosevelt will object very much to our desisting from running the convoys now. The Russians are in heavy action and will expect us to run the risk, and pay the price entailed by our contribution. The United States ships are queuing up. My own feelings, mingled with anxiety, is that the next convoy ought to sail on the 18th. The operation is justified if a half gets through. Failure on our part to make the attempt would weaken our influence with our major Allies. There are always uncertainties of weather and luck which may aid us. I share your misgivings, but I feel it is a matter of duty.

But the price of honouring such agreements was to fall most heavily upon the officers and men of warships and merchant ships in the succeeding convoys.

In North Russia, the news of the sinking of *Trinidad* came as a great shock to *Edinburgh* survivors at the Polyarnoe and Vaenga camps, chiefly as a result of the loss of some of their shipmates but also that a brand new cruiser with all the latest in gunnery defence could have fallen victim to air attack. The staggering report was at first dismissed as wild rumour but within a few hours the news was confirmed through the senior British naval officer Rear-Admiral Bevan. Its confirmation rapidly served to intensify the apprehension felt by everyone about the chances of survival when their own turn came to cross the Barents Sea to Iceland. In the meantime they did what they could to keep as fit as possible and to entertain themselves. Conditions, however, tended to deteriorate rather than improve both for the British and for the Russians.

General Frolov, commanding the 14th Soviet Army, was now making his counter attack against the Germans in the nearby port of Petsamo but the assault was repulsed with heavy losses. Hundreds of casualties were brought back to the general hospital at Murmansk and as a consequence wards and corridors were congested with wounded soldiers and the Allied wounded had to be moved out. They were transferred to the camps at Vaenga and Polyarnoe, where despite crowded conditions room had to be made. The *Edinburgh* men moved their sleeping quarters closer together to provide accommodation for the incoming wounded. When they arrived the sight that met their eyes was horrifying. Most had amputations, some still festering with gangrene. Two men had arms and legs amputated to the trunk. As leading seaman Arthur Bailey (radar) reported.

There were no orderlies, no nurses or sick bay staff to nurse them and a sort of naval barrack routine was set up with duty sections to do the best they could for the men. Difficulties arose when the wounded wanted to reach the toilet. In the case of the two men without arms or legs, it was found not easy to stop them falling over. This was overcome by making a chair seat, putting two poles through and strapping the man in. There was one very big fellow, an Egyptian, with a smashed thigh completely encased in plaster from the hip down. Each time he wanted to go to the toilet he had to be carried the two hundred yards over rough ground; an enormous effort. And there was the cabin boy David with feet still wrapped in bandages who was carried on the backs of the *Edinburgh* men, everywhere they went.

The fund-raising sale, which later became known as the 'Grand Auction', took place a week after their arrival at the camps. When the names of those killed in action were officially listed it was decided to set up a fund for the benefit of the relatives. In the middle of a snow-covered field, a chair was brought on which the auctioneer, a petty officer, stood surrounded by hundreds of matloes. Once the names of those who had died had been read it became a highly emotive affair. The men listening felt so thankful to be alive they wanted to do all they could for the families. As it happened only a day or two before the ship was torpedoed the crew had been paid and most of the men had considerable amounts of cash.

Actually there was little to sell but things like cigarettes and matches, which were in short supply, changed hands for quite large sums of money. The articles were handed to the auctioneer and the cash resulting from the sale placed in the fund. They were little personal possessions, saved by men who had lost most of their kit when the ship was sunk. A packet of twenty cigarettes fetched £10. Four more cigarettes sold singly brought 8–10 shillings. A petty officer paid £2 for a match to light a cigarette he had bought for £2. One man gave £1 for a matloe's shirt. Another paid £1 to see the buyer strip in the snow and put on the shirt. A third gave £1 for being allowed to place a snow-covered hand on the shirt-buyer's back. Here in the chilling wind accompanied by light snow showers high on the slopes above Polyarnoe, the sale went on while the astonished Russians watched. Many had left the *Edinburgh* in their working clothes, overalls and jeans and with no warm clothing. Chief Petty Officer Fiddick had been lucky, clothing himself in a serge suit, overcoat, cap, jersey and a reasonable pair of shoes. As the auction progressed, the young ship's painter who was in ragged working clothes shouted, 'I'll give you £5 for your trousers'. There was some hesitation at first, as there would be no hope of a replacement. The painter then said he could have the trousers he was wearing. To a chorus of 'Get 'em down', Fiddick accepted the challenge but whilst the exchange was going on someone noticed he had

reasonable shorts and a vest. Immediately these were bid for
and he lost them too. By the time the auction was finished he
looked, to use his own words, 'like something out of a scran
bag'. But the fund benefited very considerably. Luckily for
those who had sold their wearing apparel clothing was soon
supplied by the Russian navy for all who wanted it. They
were provided with cotton underwear and blue and white
striped jerseys as worn by the Russians themselves. The
pants Fiddick had lost in the auction were replaced by long
cotton drawers tied at the ankles to keep them draught
proof.

Toilets were primitive in the extreme. It was just a big pit
with pinewood poles balanced across; their usage a most
chancy exercise. A desperate situation developed on one
occasion when a money belt laid carefully over the pole, slid
off and fell into the pit below. The rescue was only achieved
after a supreme acrobatic effort by two matloes holding the
third by the ankles and lowering him to reach it.

The officers were not without their share of entertainment. A dinner of sorts was given by Russian navy and army
officers to their British allies at Murmansk. The food was
sparse but the vodka plentiful, and during the meal toasts
were liberally drunk to heads and leaders of the govern-
ments in the Allied cause. The Russians began with 'Long
live Churchill', and the British followed with 'Long live
Stalin'. Then came a succession of toasts to 'Roosevelt', 'De
Gaulle', 'Tito', 'Timoshenko', and so on until they ran out
of names. A young lieutenant who had been sitting quietly
at the British table drinking steadily and who by this time
was hopelessly canned, staggered to his feet, waved his glass
around with a shout of, 'And what about poor old bloody
Chiang-Kai-Shek?', then slid under the table, out for the
count.

As far as the ratings were concerned, the Russians did
their best to provide entertainment. The well known Red
Army choir which after the war visited England on

numerous occasions, gave a number of concerts at the Red Hall at Murmansk and the British contingent had open invitation to all of them. Some of these evenings proved memorable. The choir comprised about thirty singers, and often the final item, a rendering of the 'Volga Boatmen', brought the audience to their feet in appreciation. Perhaps the environment and circumstances coloured the event but it was generally accepted that no one had heard this national song sung so well. On another occasion, a number of British naval officers were invited to a Russian version of 'Rose Marie'. During the interval the tenor came to the front of the curtain and sang the song in English. As the refrain ended the Russian audience rose, turned in the direction of their English guests and much to their embarrassment, clapped heartily.

Lack of food continued to be the most serious problem but there were odd occasions when the meal, consisting of a concoction of rice or millet which was boiled with pieces of mouldy yak meat and black bread, reached comparatively banquet proportions.

There was one memorable episode when the *Edinburgh* men found a piece of corned beef lying on each plate. In recognition, all hands stood and cheered lustily. With the Merchant Navy survivors, other problems, apart from lack of food, became apparent as time went on. It was noticed that lower deck survivors, especially those from other nations, assumed that their officers no longer had authority over them and the morale of both officers and men suffered in consequence. Once landed in North Russia, every factor that might have helped to restore morale was lacking. Discipline, occupation, even their uniforms and to some extent their identities had disappeared. The result was seen in large numbers of men loitering in the streets of Murmansk, hanging about gloomy hospitals with shaved heads and dressed in miscellaneous assortments of garments which themselves went far to remove the supports of crumbling self-respect. Boredom, vodka and hope deferred were usually added to their initial trials until they could be accommodated in homeward-bound ships. Unorganised and frustrated, it was a time of moral and psychological deterioration.

Even the *Edinburgh* men were faced with the two unattractive prospects of either existing in the cold, uninviting circumstances of Russian camp life or of facing the perils of the homeward voyage in which the chances of survival were not high.

Early in June, the destroyer *Martin* after barely surviving the latest convoy run to Murmansk, made her way up through the Kola inlet and tied up alongside the jetty at Vaenga. During the voyage, the convoy had been under constant attack from enemy aircraft and U boats which had claimed seven merchant ships with great loss of life. The *Martin* had been in the forefront of the engagements, firing her guns and dropping depth charges until every unit of ammunition was used up. Although tired, exhausted and bettered there was little respite, for on arrival orders were received for their immediate return to Iceland. By arrangements with the Senior British Naval Officer, Murmansk, the captain of *Martin* agreed to take a maximum of ten *Edinburgh* survivors as passengers for the return trip. From the camp at Vaenga ten ratings were selected but were warned that on the voyage home the destroyer would be utterly defenceless against attack, having no ammunition, torpedoes or depth charges left. In view of the high risk involved they were given the opportunity to refuse if they so wished.

Despite the odds, the ten accepted and having packed up their few belongings set off for the ship. The selection proved a great disappointment to a close friend and messmate of the party, a man called Wallis, who by all accounts could no longer accept the adverse conditions of Russian camp life. Prepared to accept the risks of the return voyage he accompanied his friends to the ship, ostensibly to bid them farewell, but unseen by the sentries managed to smuggle himself aboard, hiding in a lifeboat under a tarpaulin. That night, *Martin* left the safety of the Kola inlet and moved out into the U boat infested waters of the Barents Sea, depending solely on her speed to bring her through the enemy controlled waters between Norway and Bear Island. The *Martin*, like her sister ship the *Marne*, was a new destroyer with the most up-to-date powerful engines and once outside the inlet the throttle was maintained wide open at 32 knots all the way home. As one of the Yorkshire passengers described it, 'It were full speed and down back side'.

For the stowaway it was a rough passage. About two hundred miles out the ship encountered a storm. Destroyers are notorious for heaving and pitching in rough seas and the *Martin* was no exception. Within the confines of the lifeboat Wallis was tossed and flung in all directions. Cold, black and blue from bruising and with water pouring in through a gap in the tarpaulin, his hiding place at last became untenable. Unseen by the officers, his friends pulled him from the boat and brought him into the warmth and security of the messdeck. Here, with the discreet co-operation of *Martin*'s crew, he was kept undetected until they reached Iceland. Once there, he was transferred with his colleagues on to another ship bound for the UK without anyone being the wiser. The incident must have constituted one of the very rare occasions in modern Royal Naval history when anyone became a stowaway in a warship.

Although everything possible was done to keep men occupied and entertained within the camps, there were occasions when tempers became frayed and simmering dislikes flamed into open conflict. Two seamen who were constantly engaged in this fluctuating cold and hot war were a man from Exeter and another from Glasgow. They really hated one another and would settle their differences by going outside in the snow and knocking each other senseless. As neither would surrender the fight would go on until they were unable to stand and then both would have to be carried back to their beds to slowly recover. Neither seemed to suffer any permanent damage but the encounters certainly cleared the air for a while and allowed a tolerable relationship. Within a few days they would be outside again, engaging in another blood letting exercise. Officers turned a blind eye to the fights and rightly so for they served as a valve to pent-up feelings.

To keep several hundred men under control with little or nothing to do proved a constant problem to executive officers responsible for behaviour. Impromptu concerts, sing-songs and whist drives were all employed as occupational diversions and when these forms of entertainment were not to hand, they usually embarked on a 'rodent massacre'. The huts were infested with mice and as soon as the place quieted down scores of the creatures would come swarming around the floor and scrambling over the beds. The men armed themselves with sticks and at a signal would jump out of bed and begin a mad chase around the hut, accompanied by shouts, yells and a generous delivery of ripe naval language. In the balance of life-extermination on the one hand and the high proportion of cuts, strains and bruises on the other, the mice appear to have won.

By now the Russian offensive by General Frolov against Petsamo was slowing down into a static situation but the price for the assault was shown by the growing number of casualties. The Murmansk hospital became impossibly overcrowded and although other make-shift hospitals were organized to try to cope with the situation there was a lamentable shortage of medical staff. Casualties arrived daily. An *Edinburgh* survivor, Brian Carvellas, who had to spend some weeks at the hospital before being transferred to Polyarnoe, described the situation as follows.

Hospital conditions were just bloody horrible. They had to put two wounded to a bed, one with his head alongside the other's feet. One Russian with a shattered face just lay with nothing being done for him, as patient as a dog.

Casualties were laid in rows in corridors and in little niches under stairs. There was always the danger the hospital would be hit by bombs and we knew if this happened, the result would be catastrophic.

Such was the shortage of staff by this time the original policy adopted by the Russians, that no British medical assistance would be permitted, was waived. Some British doctors and a few naval sick-bay staff were eventually allowed to assist, but with no anaesthetic available they were forced to use their own meagre supplies, snatched from *Edinburgh* before she sunk. The only deadening treatment at hand was the truth drug Pentathol, which simply produced a drunken state while the patient was undergoing the operation.

Sick-berth attendant Ted Dennerly, who assisted on these occasions, explained that the language barrier was overcome with the assistance of two Russian newspaper girl reporters who had previously worked in the Ukraine. Porters and bearers were supplied from Russian naval personnel who could not be employed on ships because there were so few available. Another factor which aggravated the situation was the arrival of many hundreds of merchant navy survivors from the ill-fated convoys PQ16 and PQ17, which had sustained such heavy losses. It was estimated that at least another 1000 men arrived in North Russia, including a considerable number of wounded. It placed the Russians in a most desperate situation. Hospital facilities, food and sheltered accommodation was already stretched beyond the limit of their reduced capabilities but somehow the challenge was met and quarters provided, basic and overcrowded though they were.

Early in June the destroyer *Martin*'s sister ship, the *Marne*, set out from the Kola inlet with more returning survivors. Modern, fast and powerfully armed her voyage westward was uneventful until she reached the area between Bear Island and North Norway. There a lone ship was encountered moving eastward. At first it was thought she might be a stray British convoy freighter and *Marne* altered course to the south to investigate. All the indications supported this assumption as it was highly unlikely that a German merchant ship would be so far north. German freighters normally hugged the Norwegian coastline relying on the protection of the Nazi air force and naval bases along the seaboard, but as *Marne* approached there were certain features which contradicted this. She was indeed a merchant ship but moving east she should have been heavy-laden and low in the water. Instead her plimsol line was high and clearly unladen. Empty British ships did not travel towards Russia but away from it.

With some caution the destroyer approached. Suddenly a flag was run up the mast revealing her identity, and as she turned it was seen she was an armed German merchant ship. *Marne* had barely recovered from the surprise when the German opened fire. A salvo of shells fell all around the ship without scoring a direct hit but as the destroyer circled rapidly away a barrage of shrapnel fell over the decks crowded with crew and *Edinburgh* passengers. Within minutes *Marne* was out of range, standing off from the German and checking her casualties. There were many killed and wounded and among the dead were a number of *Edinburgh* men. Oddly enough it had been a strangely uncomplicated incident in this war of killing and being killed but as the men on the decks of *Marne* bent over their torn, wounded shipmates they saw it as cold bloody murder. Until this moment, there had been no real hatred of the enemy. True he was feared and treated with respect as a highly trained worthwhile opponent and if you didn't kill him, he would kill you. But this was somehow different. Sorrow and distress became fused with a deep anger and a loathing of their attackers. Men vented their wrath in a tirade of cursing and their pity in an unashamed coursing of tears.

At *Marne*'s stern the sea boiled white as the propellors trembled to increased revolutions. The destroyer swept round in a tight circle, closing the German at speed preparing to attack. Almost inaudible above the babble of voices on deck, the vibrating hull, the humming of fans and dynamos and the chatter of water against the ship's side, the metallic tones of the loud-speakers rasped out preliminary orders from the bridge for the port torpedo tubes to be made ready giving course, speed and direction. There was a sudden flurry of activity as the torpedo crew swung into action, the drone of the revolving turntable as the tubes trained outboard, their gaping mouths pointing evilly against the white wash streaming past from the destroyer's creaming bows. The German ship, seemingly all too aware that its destruction was imminent, was now firing erratically in a spirit of desperation. Gunnery control appeared to have been abandoned for unregulated panic shooting. The shell splashes, now falling far wide of the mark, presented no immediate danger to the destroyer and she sped on relentlessly. Well within firing range, *Marne* swung away to starboard presenting the port torpedo crew with the target on which they could now line up. The men along the destroyer's decks watched in silence, faces inscrutable, without pity in their hearts, waiting.

Then with almost startling suddeness, the loudspeakers clanged once more into life. Perhaps the mechanical process of transmission camouflaged emotion but the order of execution from the bridge seemed to come with ice-cold deliberation, betraying neither passion nor excitement, 'Fire one!' Immediately, there was the familiar click of the tripping lever, the shrouded roar in the explosion chamber, the high pitched hiss of compressed air and then with almost startling clarity the torpedo was on its way, its silver sleekness gleaming fractionally in the cold air above the water before it plunged into the surface of the sea. 'Fire two!' Again the tubes shuddered, and the second was in the water following along the trail of its leader. The men watched fascinated as the turbulent wakes of foaming bubbles, clear against the dark water, vanished as the speeding torpedoes neared the doomed ship. Both were on target. The enemy ship, shuddering under the impact, slewed around and stopped, the centre of the hull completely blown away.

There was no violent explosion. The bridge superstructure slowly collapsed and settled into the water down through the midship decking. In minutes she began to turn wearily on to her side, with men swarming along the tilting decks clinging desperately to anything, to stop them sliding into the scuppers. Others were already jumping or diving into the sea. Only two minutes later she was gone, leaving a great pool of bubbling water, oil, wreckage and a hundred or more men gasping and struggling in the icy water. In an extremity of fear and exhaustion, crying for help, they tried to swim towards the British destroyer. Very slowly *Marne* moved in. Scrambling nets were lowered over the side to speed up and simplify the rescue operation. As they neared, some men were shouting hysterically, others swam in silence preserving what little strength they had, a number sank quickly without fuss before they could be reached. One by one they clambered up the netting. A stubborn few, braggardly taking their time, were hauled unceremoniously aboard and dumped like sacks of wet coal upon the steel deck.

Stopped in broad daylight, a little north of the 72nd parallel midway between North Cape, Norway and Bear Island, it was no place for a British warship. Tension mounted as the crew tried to hasten the rescue operation, cursing the men who took their time laboriously climbing the netting. They had every right to be anxious. Any U boat within five miles could have seen them against the skyline and the risk they were taking was frightening. If the enemy didn't get them now they never would. All the while the radar arm swept ceaselessly around the dark screen, watching for aircraft or ships that might be out of sight over the edge of the horizon. The asdic dome in the bottom of the ship pinged its endless note, searching for a lurking submarine. And in the meantime the long slow job of recovering the enemy from the sea went on while the ship rolled silently in the swell and the black water slapped against the hull.

Already there were bodies, lifejacketed but motionless; the cold had killed them quickly. There would be no time for the dead, little enough for the living. Indeed, throughout the ship as tension increased, there was an awareness that they had already used up their quota of luck. Yet there were still some thirty or forty men in the sea at the ship's side waiting their turn to climb the net. And then, as if the moment they dreaded had been born out of an anticipation from which they had shrunk, the loudspeaker from the asdic cabinet clicked into action. The voice of the operator was urgent compelling, 'Asdic – bridge, asdic – bridge. I have an echo red 90, sir. Three miles. Strong and closing fast.' Even as the words died, the emergency action stations bell clanged its piercing note throughout the ship. Already alert, the crew were closed up to their posts in less than a minute. There was a sudden vibration through the hull as the engines began to turn the screws, followed by the chilling but vital order from the bridge, 'Remove scrambling nets'. Some of the Germans were half-way up the net as *Marne* moved off, increasing speed with every passing second. The cries and screams of the men left struggling in the water defied description. *Marne* had done what she could. The alternative, to carry on picking up the remainder and become a sitting target for the approaching U boat was unthinkable. No doubt the captain remembered how the destroyer *Matabele*, only six months earlier, had in these same waters been hit by a torpedo which plunged into the magazine. The ship had disintegrated in an enormous flash and only one rating had been saved out of the entire crew of two hundred. The captain was determined this should not happen to *Marne*. And crammed with survivors, he had no intention of hanging around engaging in what could result as a fruitless hunt for the U boat. The earlier precipitate hatred of the German crew was now somewhat defused by a feeling of pity for those they had to leave behind. Unless the approaching U boat could reach them in time they would all die.

In minutes, *Marne* was advancing westward, enormous waves creaming back from her slender bows and exhibiting that dramatic quality of power and speed which was the pride of the modern destroyer. Quickly the bobbing heads of the Germans became mere specks on the surface and were soon out of sight altogether. But even when *Marne* reached the safety of Iceland, bearing the bodies of her crew and those of the *Edinburgh* men who had been killed on her decks, the cries of the Germans they had left struggling in the water were still ringing in their ears.

CHAPTER 12

The *Niger* Tragedy

IT WAS NOT UNTIL SEPTEMBER 1942, that the last of the *Edinburgh* survivors returned to Britain. During the intervening period the men were sent back in groups, according to the availability of accommodation in Royal Naval warships or freighters in homeward-bound convoys. One typical example of this was given by Reg Phillips.

My turn to be sent home came in July, when I joined a small party who were taken round to the White Sea port of Archangel, which at that period of the year was free from ice. We travelled in a flower class corvette and there joined a Panamanian merchant ship. We looked forward to the prospect of possibly getting some Virginian cigarettes but were very surprised when the crew asked us for some. The ship proved to be one of the convoy we had escorted to Russia some months before, and had been frozen in all winter. They said they were very short of supplies, but believe me, we thought we were in the lap of luxury after the food and conditions we had endured during the last three months. Such was our longing for cigarettes, we organized searches of the ship for fag-ends, which we made up into smokes for each other, until we eventually smoked all the fag-ends of the fag-ends! The ship's company was made up of all nationalities, including Americans who had wanted to do their bit for Britain before their own country had entered the war. Our own petty officer was in charge of the party and we were each given a job. I was appointed Vicker's machine gunner, but apart from one or two scares we had a fairly quiet trip home.

After reaching Iceland, we left the convoy and made our way independently to Loch Ewe in Scotland. The chief engineer was pleased to be free of the restrictive speed of the convoy of 8 knots and was really proud to extract $10\frac{1}{2}$ knots from the engines of his ancient vessel. George, the greaser, had never left the USA before and was looking forward with great expectations to his first visit to the UK. He would entertain us when off duty, sitting in his cabin with the door open, scratching out a familiar tune on his fiddle. We went through the boom at Loch Ewe early one morning and called George up from the engine room to get his first glimpse of the UK. He gazed round the loch side and the mountains in wonderment and finally exploded, 'Say, where's all the goddam cities?'

In late June a large group of *Edinburgh* men were alerted they would be returning with the homeward convoy QP13. Again the familiar apprehensions emerged as those susceptible to even the most tenuous associations with superstition considered the ominous number. They certainly had grounds for pessimism. During the last three months *Trinidad* had been torpedoed, *Edinburgh* sunk, and finally *Trinidad* sent to the bottom, and in each engagement the number 13 had related to the enterprise. Was this convoy QP13 also to be added to the list of tragedies?

The convoy of 35 merchant ships set out from the Kola inlet on 27 June. Its escort was made up of 5 destroyers, *Inglefield, Achates, Volunteer, Intrepid* and *Garland*; 4 corvettes, *Stalwort, Honeysuckle, Hyderabad* and *Roseleys*; 2 minesweepers, *Niger* and *Hussar*; and the two trawlers *Lady Madeline* and *St Elstan*.

Edinburgh officers and ratings, selected for the homeward voyage, were distributed among the escort vessels according to the availability of accommodation. Approximate figures suggest that an average of 30 were alloted to each of the destroyers and corvettes, about 40 each to the minesweepers and 16 each to the trawlers. An overall total figure approaching 400. A British submarine had also been assigned to accompany the convoy and even here four places were set aside, a form of transport which at the time was considered the safest way to get back to England.

During the embarkation allocations to the various ships meant that men with longstanding friendships were now split up. Urgent endeavours were made to alter arrangements to enable them to be together for the voyage home. All these applications were refused, the grouping strictly adhered to. Unknown to them at the time, these decisions proved to be the critical verdict between life and death. The convoy had an uneventful passage to Iceland, partly because it ran into fog but mainly because the enemy had concentrated the whole of its attack on the eastward bound convoy, the ill-fated PQ17, of which 24 of the 33 ships were eventually sunk. On 4 July the convoy arrived off the north eastern corner of Iceland and divided as arranged. 16 of the 35 ships bound for the United Kingdom turned due south along Iceland's east coast. The remaining 19, mostly American bound for Reykjavik, made their way along the north-east coast led by Captain John Hiss, master of the American freighter *Robin*, to whom had been delegated the responsibility of acting commodore for this last leg of the voyage. The bad weather which had accompanied them for the greater part of the voyage now ceased to be a protective shroud and became instead a matter of grave concern.

Weather conditions had prevented all ships from calculating their whereabouts by astronomical observations and now the convoy had only a rough idea of their position. Unknown to the commodore and captains of the merchant ships, a British minefield had been laid off the north-west corner of Iceland in an attempt to catch any German warships trying to break out through the Denmark Straits into the Atlantic to attack Allied shipping. This left a narrow channel, ten miles wide, lying between the southern rim of the minefield and the Icelandic coastline through which the ships had to pass.

It was a stormy evening, with a northerly wind tumbling low clouds down to almost sea-level and gale rain reducing visibility to about one mile. By 7 o'clock that evening the minesweeper *Niger* commanded by the senior officer of the escort group, Commander Antony Cubison, RN, went on ahead in order to obtain a navigational fix, requesting the acting commodore to reform his ships from five columns into two to negotiate the narrow passage. From soundings, Cubison estimated that the North Cape of Iceland had been passed and ordered a south-west course to try to make a landfall. Cautiously making his way through the mist and cloud he suddenly saw what appeared to be a steep cliff looming up in the murk, which he thought must be the North Cape after all. It seemed that the convoy had altered course too soon and if they maintained the direction they would be into the coastline. To correct this, Cubison immediately signalled Captain Hiss to bring the convoy back on to a west course. During this period of reduced visibility ships had been streaming fog-buoys, a simple procedure adopted to prevent a following ship hitting the stern of the vessel ahead. A rope, attached to a floating buoy is towed behind the leading ship and this in turn throws up a column of water which can be detected. But hardly had the convoy swung back on to the new course when a clearance in the weather showed that what had been taken for a cliff was in fact a large iceberg. Cubison, realizing his mistake and well aware they could be close to or even in the minefield, hastily signalled the convoy to alter course to the south-west.

But it was too late. At exactly 10.40 p.m. *Niger* herself ran on to a mine and blew up. From the decks of the trawler *St*

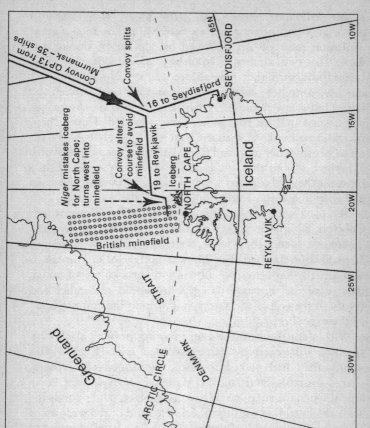

HMS *Niger* with convoy strays into British minefield 4 July 1942

Elstan following some 300 yards away, the *Edinburgh* passengers and the trawler crew watched in horror as a great explosion rent the air, followed by a pillar of smoke and flame. In one almost involuntary movement the ships behind and on either side sheared away. *Niger* sank very quickly. With her bottom torn out and her back broken she lasted but a few minutes. As she settled into the Arctic sea there was a muffled roar as her boilers exploded. And then, maintaining her level with the water, she slowly heeled over on to her side, her mast and funnel dipping despairingly into a surface of burning oil gushing from her tanks. For a moment the keel showed wet black against the turbulent sea and then in a rush of vomiting bubbles she was gone.

She took with her her commanding officer, Commander Cubison, 80 officers and crew, and 39 *Edinburgh* passengers. There was silence for a while, a sickening, terrifying silence as realization dawned that this was no fearful nightmare, it was actually happening. A horrifying mass killing of which they were the witnesses; they who would remember and testify to the end of their days, confirming the completeness of the execution.

Within and beneath the ever growing pool of black evil-smelling oil licked by flame lay their friends, men with whom they had played football, exchanged confidences, shared grumbles and laughed together. Men who at Poly-arnoe, when the auction sale had taken place, paid pounds for a worthless trinket to subscribe to the fund of the widows of those who had died in *Edinburgh*. Now in a brief moment of time they had themselves become the victims of a war that was merciless, inhuman and brutal; killed, ironically, by devices which had been designed and placed to destroy the enemy. It was these which by a quirk of fate had become their very executioner. Standing on the rain-soaked decks, stunned into a tight-lipped muteness, they were now the mourners, separated by their own thoughts but bound by the same shock, the same awesome sorrow. Some asked themselves whether number 13 had upheld its sinister reputation.

Moments later a freighter, the SS *Hybert*, hit a mine. A great flash lit the sky as almost in two she disappeared within seconds leaving a cauldron of burning oil spewing across the surface. Wild confusion broke out as among the following convoy one ship after another was shaken by heavy explosions. Each eruption triggered off other mines nearby, throwing up huge columns of water making them appear like shell splashes. In the running seas and the poor visibility the masters of the freighters, unaware of the existence of the minefield, readily assumed they were being shelled by a distant German warship or being attacked by U boats. They had no idea which way to turn for the explosions seemed all round them. A few minutes later another merchant ship, the SS *Heffron*, blew up followed by the SS *Marramar*, leaving their crews fighting for survival in the icy water or clinging to rafts. The SS *John Randolph* became the next victim. Severely damaged she managed to remain afloat, her bows blown off but the inner bulkheads holding the rush of incoming seas. Within minutes confusion was total. The time to signal intentions was gone. It was every ship for herself, claiming the right for survival, sluggishly twisting and turning in a desperate bid to avoid the unknown terror that lay in ambush waiting to strike. The bulky freighters, clumsy, agonisingly slow in movement, yawed around without any positive direction, their captains cursing other vessels turning across their path while a chorus of sirens added further panic to an already chaotic situation.

And then only 400 yards away on the starboard bow, another blinding flash lit up the murky grey of the Arctic night, followed by a violent explosion. This was the Russian freighter *Rodina*. Slewing round in a tight turn to port the mine had slammed against her hull about half-way along the starboard side. Instantly tons of water rushed into the gaping hole, smashing through weakened bulkheads and watertight doors fractured by the eruption, pulling her down into the grey black sea. Within seconds she began to list to starboard, still slewing round until her tilted decks were exposed to the other ships. Slowly her rails dipped under, sliding further and further into the sea, her decks filled with people sliding and slipping down the canted platform, struggling, fighting to reach the lifeboats. There were many women and even a few children among them. Two lifeboats drifted away empty, yet supported some twenty or thirty in the water with hands locked over the gunwhales.

Hardly had the echoes of the *Rodina* explosion died, when the freighter immediately astern, the SS *Exterminator* ran on to a mine. This time there was no smoke or fire, just a muffled detonation that ripped out her middle and broke her in half. Her end was swift and certain. V-shaped, her stern and bow hung suspended above the water for a few moments, spilling its cargo of human flotsam and black oil, and then in a roar of exploding boilers as the two parts up-ended she disappeared, leaving only a mass of white churning water in the middle of an area of black oil fuel and struggling men.

By now, the living and the dead in the sea numbered well over four hundred. With the loss of *Niger* and 6 merchant ships sunk out of nineteen, the two 'pick-up' trawlers, *St Elstan* and *Lady Madeline*, in the middle of the holocaust, were also unaware of the existence of the British minefield. They assumed that a pack of U boats somewhere around them was firing spreads of torpedoes into the centre of the convoy. The remaining 14 freighters were still floundering around, not knowing which way to turn. More could be sunk at any moment and with the destroyers and most of the corvettes well ahead an immediate decision had to be made to protect the remaining vessels. The decision, when it came, brought with it a nightmare of horror. As the *St*

Elstan swept into the middle of the devastated area, a spread of depth charges rocketed from the ship, hurling the deadly containers far out over the water. At the same time, a number were dropped from astern.

At varying distances from the trawler there were people swimming or trying to swim through the oil-covered surface. People in the last stages of exhaustion who seeing the ship raised an arm in hope of rescue, people terror-stricken, screaming for help. Scores of bodies lay prone on the surface, or lifebelted sat in the water with unseeing eyes. Suddenly with a volley of ear-splitting crashes the depth charges exploded, shooting columns of foaming water high into the air. The effect on the people in the sea was horrific, shocking beyond conception. The lucky ones died instantly but for the rest. . . .

As far as the *St Elstan* was concerned, it was assumed that the depth-charging would keep the U boats submerged for a while, at least to give them time to pick up those who might still be alive. Steadily, thoroughly, they began their search totally unaware they were moving around in the middle of a minefield. Scrambling nets were lowered and efforts to rescue the living begun. That anyone should be alive at all seemed almost beyond belief. But miraculously there were those who had survived the sinking, the cold and the depth-charging. Among these were two *Edinburgh* men, the sole survivors from *Niger*. Some in the thickness of the oil had lived through the worst. But for men in the sea oil is a vicious, iniquitous thing. It burns the eyes, scorches the lungs and tears the stomach in violent outbursts of retching.

One of the *Edinburgh* survivors taking passage home in the *St Elstan* was Harry Cook. In a bid to help save those in the water he went over the side in the scrambling net hanging by one hand, while trying to pull in survivors with the other. One of the trawler's gun crew hung over the side with him. Cook describes what happened.

We brought in a total of 16 altogether. The trawler was going around in circles trying to pick them up but many could not be reached. The waves kept sweeping them out of our grasp. It was a grim ordeal, as some of those in the water were women and children. These were the families of the Russian and Polish consul staff taking passage to Britain. I remember picking up a small child from the water, finding it dead and letting it drop back into the sea. Some were able to climb up the netting themselves but all were soaked in oil, their eyes sealed and blinded and so utterly spent and on the verge of collapse, they could do nothing to help themselves. During the rescue, a huge wave caught us both and tore us off the net, away from the ship, but the next wave carried us crashing back on to the ship's side and the netting, which we managed to grab. The skipper was furious, 'Get back aboard and that's an order'. We came across a boat with a few Russians in. They managed to climb aboard on their own but left one man sitting alone in the boat, stark staring mad, shouting and screaming in his native language. We managed to get him aboard eventually and laid him on the deck, where he continued with his hysterical outburst. The Russians were so ashamed that one of their own countrymen should behave in this way, they went over and kicked him in the ribs while he was lying there.

In the meantime some of the other escorts had arrived and began to pick up survivors. Among these, was the Free French corvette *Roselys*, under the command of Lieutenant Bergeret, which with the trawler *Lady Madeline* and the *St Elstan* steamed about in the middle of the minefield for six-and-a-half hours with complete disregard for their own safety, rescuing survivors. Between them they picked up 230, some of whom in the following hours died of exposure.

Later, Lieutenant Bergeret was told by Vice-Admiral Braynard, commander of the American Task Force, that he had earned 'the respect and gratitude of the United States Navy', for during the time the *Roselys* had remained in the minefield the ship had saved 170 men and women. A sad reminder of the number who died after being picked up can be seen from the following signal.

Unless otherwise ordered, *Roselys* and *Lady Madeline* intend to proceed independently to Reykjavik at maximum speed, to land injured survivors from *Exterminator, Rodina, Hybert, Marramar, Heffron, Randolph* and *Niger*. Survivors are distributed as follows:
Roselys – 120 including 6 injured.
St Elstan – 23 no injured.
Lady Madeline – 40 including one injured.
ETA *Roselys* 1630 GMT.

From this it appears that 47 had died after being rescued.

Meanwhile, the 16 ships of the port wing of the convoy which had earlier detached from the main body were making their way along the eastern coastline of Iceland to reach Seydisfiord. Weather conditions were atrocious, with visibility down to less than a mile and no opportunity to get a bearing to shape their course. In desperation, the destroyer *Inglefield* despatched a signal to her sister ship *Intrepid*, 'Where do you make your position?' To which came the reply, 'Half way up Mount Fountain'. Eventually the convoy arrived safely at Seydisfiord but were immediately told to refuel and proceed to sea to escort the battle fleet which were out looking for the German battleship *Tirpitz*. This great ship was a source of constant anxiety to the chiefs of staff of British Naval Operations trying to protect convoys to North Russia. Based in Norwegian waters, she constantly imposed a threat to sea communications. The presence of the *Tirpitz* at Trondheim in Norway was a matter of deep concern to Mr Winston Churchill, who in a minute to the chiefs of staff a few months earlier, wrote.

> The destruction or even the crippling of this ship is the greatest event at sea at the present time. No other target is comparable to it. Even if she were only crippled it would be difficult to take her back to Germany.... The entire naval situation throughout the world would be altered, and the naval command in the Pacific would be regained.... The whole strategy of the war turns at this period on this ship, which is holding four times the number of British ships paralysed.

The *Tirpitz* scare at this time was real enough. The German battle fleet had actually set out from Altenfiord in North Norway to attack the PQ17 convoy moving eastward to Murmansk. The enemy force comprised the great *Tirpitz* of 43,000 tons with eight 15-inch, twelve 6-inch and sixteen 4-inch guns and carrying 6 aircraft; the pocket battleship *Admiral Scheer* of 12,000 tons with six 11-inch, eight 6-inch and six 4-inch guns and two aircraft; the large battle cruiser *Hipper* of 14,000 tons with eight 8-inch, twelve 4-inch and 3 aircraft; and an escort screen of 8 destroyers. These were the circumstances and the factors which formed the decision to send *Inglefield* and the accompanying destroyers to sea again. The German naval force was in fact recalled by the German Naval Command after being at sea only 10 hours after confirmation that the scattered PQ17 convoy had been almost annihilated by their aircraft.

Edinburgh survivor Arthur Bailey who was taking passage in *Inglefield* at the time, says.

> Having arrived at Seydisfiord, we were ordered to refuel as quickly as possible and proceed to sea. The captain sent a signal to the naval officer in charge which read, 'I have *Edinburgh* survivors aboard and

intend keeping them with me. They would be useful in case of any nonsense with the *Tirpitz*.' Immediately came the reply, 'No, these people have had enough – land them!' It was a great relief, for after all we had been through, we were in no condition to go out and fight another battle. And so we came ashore, where the army looked after us for about a week, until the destroyers *Martin* and *Marne* came in and took us back to the UK on 14 July.

The arrival back in Britain of small groups of *Edinburgh* survivors brought about a variety of incidents which are well worth recording. Their appearance readily captured the attention of onlookers wherever they went. Straight from the camps in North Russia, they wore Russian fur caps, balaclava helmets, old jerseys, Russian naval gear and old coats. Most were unshaven and many stones lighter than when they were last in the country. Leonard Bradley recalls they had to change trains at Paddington for Plymouth. He says.

I was wearing Russian clothing and an old fur hat and on my size six feet were size eleven ski boots padded with rags. We all went into a pub at the station at about 6 o'clock in the evening and noticed everybody staring at us. When I gave the landlord a badly stained pound note he said, 'What's this then?' I told him it was oil fuel and he said, 'I'm keeping this'. He gave me another for it and added, 'Drinks are on the house'. On the train journey down to Plymouth the ticket collector came along the corridor asking, 'Is there anyone here by the name of Leading Stoker Bradley?' When I told him I was, he said, 'You're a friend of Jimmy Brown. The driver of this train is his father. What happened to him? All his parents have had is a telegram reporting him as missing.' I told him, 'You can take it from me, the poor lad is dead – he died alongside me in the ship.' When we arrived at North Road Station a smaller engine was put on to shunt us into the docks and I never had a chance to speak to the driver, who must have brought that train all the way to Plymouth knowing his son was dead.

William Wallis and his messmates arrived in Scotland and while waiting for their train, found the NAAFI canteen open. After three months of near starvation they were ready to eat anything. One of the party who was crazy about peaches managed to find enough money to buy a tin. He ripped it open and ate the lot. Minutes later he was on his back rolling in agony. His stomach wouldn't take it. He suddenly brought them up the same as they came out of the tin. There was a cockney standing by looking on in amazement. He said, 'Blimey, it's the first time I've ever seen a sailor sick in port.'

Alan Devoud, who was Captain Faulkner's writer, ever remembers his arrival in the UK.

We arrived at Scapa Flow and then transferred to the little town of Thurso in north Scotland. The town hall or part of it, had been transferred into a sort of transit station. It was a Sunday, the last in August and the catering was handled by a party of WRENS. Shortly after arrival, we were ushered into a large room with long tables and benches, and there to our great joy, a meal waiting. For all of us, it was the first real meal after the months of starvation in Russia. It had been four months since we had had our last full meal on board *Edinburgh* on the 30th April. The roast beef and Yorkshire pudding of that dinner are engraved on my memory until my dying day. Although the hall was crowded, the only sound to be heard was that of knives and forks on plates. What food can mean to starving men! After the meal, we had to wait until evening for the train to Plymouth. Near the town hall was a public garden. The weather was fine and all we could do was to lie on the grass, incapable of moving, our bellies seemingly on the point of bursting. On the long journey from Thurso to Plymouth, the train stopped at Crewe, and as with other stations, civilian passengers joined. In the corridor, passing our compartment, a woman with a loud voice said to her friend, 'Don't go in there dearie, they're not nice, they're sailors.' You can imagine – we were pretty indignant.

At Plymouth, the carriages were switched to a side track and slowly shunted into Devonport. With a squeal of brakes and a loud hiss of escaping steam the train ground to a stop at the tiny halt within the confines of Devonport dockyard. Carriage doors swung open wide and on to the platform shuffled the men of *Edinburgh*, weary, gaunt, but eyes alight with excitement and a heart filled with thankfulness to be home at last.

As they marched away towards the parade ground of the nearby Royal Naval barracks of HMS *Drake*, they gazed about them at the familiar surroundings of dockyard activity. Here, alongside the wharves and basins lay the ships that fought the battles of the sea and had so far survived. The jetties were full, overfull. They lay three or four abreast in places. Stem to stern, a forest of masts reached for the sky, sharp bows mounting proudly above the level of the wharves. Wharves, which in themselves seemed crowded with wooden sheds and tin-roofed huts. Around and between them lay a jumble of giant coils of wire and rope, anchor cable and oil drums. It was the ships however that caught the eye. Lean grey destroyers, floated with almost parental dignity beside a brood of corvettes and frigates, and black faced armed trawlers. Here they rested, salt eroded and rusty, fresh from their encounters in the Arctic. It was at this time in autumn 1942, that Winston Churchill declared.

This is not the end, it is not even the beginning of the end. But, it is perhaps, the end of the beginning.

By the end of 1942 the war at sea had reached its climax. The Russian convoy route had become known as 'The Gateway to Hell'. In every naval establishment in Great Britain the words 'Russian convoy' came to be dreaded. A draft chit to join a ship at Scapa Flow could bring despondency to a sailor for the chances were high he would find himself on a ship bound for Murmansk. And there was an even greater chance he would never return.

The homecoming of *Edinburgh* survivors claimed no banner headlines. In fact they returned almost unnoticed, unheralded. It mattered little for the public have short memories anyway. Possibly the gold will be remembered far longer than the graves. But for the men of *Edinburgh*, she will be the memorial, the chronicle that will be engraved upon their hearts and minds to the end of their days.

Epilogue

SINCE THE FINAL CHAPTER of this story was written, news has been released of the successful outcome of attempts to salvage the gold bullion from HMS *Edinburgh*. During the latter part of August 1981, the 1400 ton salvage vessel *Stephaniturm*, owned by Jessop Marine Ltd, located the wreck and having fixed a position immediately over it began preparations for recovery. Previously, Jessops had pinpointed the cruiser 800 feet down and were able to confirm her identity by remote robot cameras. The video film clearly showed *Edinburgh* lying on her side in a remarkably good state of preservation after 39 years on the sea bed.

Stephaniturm is one of the world's most technically advanced diving vessels ideally equipped for the recovery of the treasure. She is so designed that from a chamber pool within her hull, a diving bell can be submerged to hang immobile above a wreck. In early September exploratory operations began in earnest. The pressurized bell with two divers inside it was lowered to a point about 50 feet directly above the cruiser. From the bell itself, one diver carrying his umbilical wires and hoses and wearing a special suit through which gallons of hot water continually circulated to combat the intensely cold sea temperature, swam down to the wreck and took a first look at the torpedo hole leading to the bomb room containing the gold bullion. He found however, that so much silt had penetrated over the years that it would be difficult to reach the treasure. As a result, a new access was made through an empty oil fuel tank adjacent to the gold room.

On 11th of September, divers successfully entered the compartment and began to remove silt and wreckage covering the gold. This proved to be a highly delicate and dangerous operation, as all around lay explosives scattered from the effect of the torpedo blast which had sunk *Edinburgh* in May 1942. But on Wednesday the 16th, diver John Rossier thrust his hand into the thick sediment on the floor and lifted a short heavy metal bar which proved to be one of the gold ingots.

In great excitement he informed the diving supervisor over the inter-com waiting in the mother ship far above on the surface of his find. For the ship's company and all those connected with the operation it was a moment of triumph. From then on the gold bars were recovered more quickly. Eventually they were loaded into metal cages and brought to the surface at an estimated load run value of £4 million each. There were believed to be about 400 bars awaiting recovery, each valued at around £100,000, to make a total of £45 million. Out of this, it is believed that about £20 million has been taken by Jessop Marine. Of the remainder, the Russians, whose gold it was in the first place, have taken two-thirds and the British Government one-third. Bared of her gold, *Edinburgh* has now returned to the calm darkness and peace of her War Grave alone with heroic memories of the past.

Bibliography

Cajus Bekker, *Hitler's Naval War* (Macdonald & Jane, 1974).

Ian Campbell, *The Kola Run* (Futura, 1975).

Brian Schofield, *The Russian Convoys* (Batsford, 1964 and Pan, 1971).

General Index

Index of Ships

Derek Wilson
The World Atlas of Treasure £6.50

Few can be so dead to the romance of history that the promise of hidden treasure does not cause them a thrill of excitement. The unbelievable magnificence buried in the tomb of Tutankhamen; the loot of the Nazis beneath the tranquil surface of an Austrian lake; the pirate's hoard hurriedly concealed beneath the sands of Hispaniola – this is the stuff of fiction and yet exists too in sober reality. In *The World Atlas of Treasure* Derek Wilson investigates the legends old and new, tells the story of the great discoveries of the past, and describes the wealth that still awaits the lucky finder.

Francis Hitching
The World Atlas of Mysteries £6.50

From the origins of the universe and terrestrial life, through the unique development of man, to the secrets of ancient civilizations and bizarre phenomena in the sky and beyond – the enormous scope of this encyclopaedia, its exhaustive research and copious illustrations (maps, photographs, diagrams) make it a unique and fascinating book. Francis Hitching, author of *Earth Magic*, is one of the world's leading authorities on the inexplicable and the unexplained.

'A book of absorbing interest to anyone who believes that there are more things in heaven and earth than science will recognize'
DR KIT PEDLER (creator of DOOMWATCH), EVENING NEWS

The Neck of the Giraffe £2.50

or Where Darwin Went Wrong

A revelation on how a once-revolutionary hypothesis became scientific dogma and how the mass of evidence that doesn't fit has opened cracks in the Darwinian explanation.

The bestselling author of *The World Atlas of Mysteries* and *Earth Magic* guides the general reader through the important new theories explaining life on earth and the tumult of debate that is spotlighted by the Darwin centenary.

Max Hastings
Bomber Command £2.95

Winner of the W. Somerset Maugham Award for Non-Fiction 1980 . . .
Bomber Command's offensive against the cities of Germany was one
of the last war's epic campaigns. Hamburg, Berlin, Dresden – the author
traces the development of area bombing, using a wealth of documents,
letters, diaries and interviews.

'Probably the most brilliant use of anecdotal material that has so far
come out of the Second World War . . . brilliant'
THE TIMES LITERARY SUPPLEMENT

'The most critical book yet written about Bomber Command . . . also far
and away the best' ECONOMIST

Elmer Bendiner
The Fall of Fortresses £1.75

August 1943: target – the vital ballbearing factories at Schweinfurt,
southern Germany. Three hundred US Eighth Air Force B17 Flying
Fortresses are sent to cripple the Nazi war machine. But across the
enemy coast the Messerschmitts are waiting. More than 100 bombers
and almost fifteen hundred men were lost in two daylight raids that
barely dented the armouries of the Reich.

'Ranks among the outstanding air memoirs of the war'
MAX HASTINGS, STANDARD

Lord Kilbracken
Bring Back My Stringbag £1.50

a Swordfish pilot at war

Vigorous, honest, at times hilarious, this account by Lord Kilbracken of
his five years in the Fleet Air Arm during the last war provides a
remarkable picture of the Swordfish aircraft (jokingly known as
'Stringbags'), seemingly 'left in the war by mistake', and the oddball
characters who flew them. The author experienced every hazard that
could confront a shipborne pilot – torpedo and bomb attacks, mines,
flak-filled skies and ditching in mid-Atlantic, coming through with his
courage and off-beat humour undaunted.

B. H. Liddell Hart
History of the Second World War £3.95

Liddell Hart brought his brilliant and original mind to this magnificent narrative of the war – a task which occupied him for over twenty years. Trenchant, searching, thought-provoking, it is military history written with realism and learning, and illuminated with flashes of insight.

'The book has the mark of the author's genius – a lucidity and insight such as no other military writer can match . . . it will long be read with profit and enjoyment by all interested in the military art' ARMY QUARTERLY

Alvin Toffler
Future Shock £1.95

Future shock is the disease of change. Its symptoms are already here . . . *Future Shock* tells what happens to people overwhelmed by too rapid change . . . And looks at the human side of tomorrow. Brilliantly disturbing, the book analyses the new and dangerous society now emerging, and shows how to come to terms with the future.

'An important book reaching some startling conclusions' BBC

'If this book is neglected we shall all be very foolish' C. P. SNOW

The Third Wave £1.95

The First Wave was the Agricultural Revolution. The Second Wave was the Industrial Revolution. The Third Wave is the mightiest wave of all. The Technological Revlolution. And it is upon us now. Alvin Toffler describes the new civilization that is being created around us – its life-styles, jobs and sexual attitudes; the family, economic and political structures. He shows how to adapt to these changes and enjoy a startling, new, and fulfilling way of life.

'All through *The Third Wave*, one comes across brilliant passages . . . Toffler's energy is awesome' THE TIMES EDUCATIONAL SUPPLEMENT

'Another blockbuster' GUARDIAN

Ian Skidmore
Lifeboat VC £1

Dick Evans is a man with 'a special sort of courage'. For over half a century he has been associated with the *Moelfre* lifeboat in Anglesey, guarding one of the most perilous stretches of British waters and taking part in some of the most dramatic rescues in recent history.

Evans is the only lifeboatman to hold two RNLI gold medals – that institution's equivalent to a Victoria Cross. These awards are amply justified as we learn of his many rescues in storms that gusted at up to 125 mph with gargantuan waves reaching heights of forty feet or more.

Bernard Levin
Taking Sides £1.95

Whether writing about the fall of Cambodia or the pitfalls of window-box gardening, Bernard Levin, now a journalistic institution, never relaxes his gift for eloquence, wit, wisdom and clear-sightedness. This is a sparkling selection of his most memorable articles from *The Times* and the *Observer* – provocative, abrasive, hilarious and inspired.

'The most remarkable journalist of our time'
PHILIP TOYNBEE, OBSERVER

'Unique, brilliant, prolific' FINANCIAL TIMES

Hugh Thomas
An Unfinished History of the World £3.95

Following the path of Herodotus, Raleigh and H. G. Wells, one of the foremost historians of the twentieth century surveys the story of humankind from the dawn of man into our own turbulent times. Revised and extended by the author for this Pan edition, including a series of newly commissioned maps.

'What richness it provides. There is scarcely an aspect of human life it does not illuminate' THE TIMES

'Hugh Thomas has laboured hugely to find and fit together all the facts and ideas that constitute not only our history, but our politics as well' ECONOMIST

Fiction

☐	**Options**	Freda Bright	£1.50p
☐	**The Thirty-nine Steps**	John Buchan	£1.50p
☐	**Secret of Blackoaks**	Ashley Carter	£1.50p
☐	**Winged Victory**	Barbara Cartland	95p
☐	**The Sittaford Mystery**	Agatha Christie	£1.00p
☐	**Dupe**	Liza Cody	£1.25p
☐	**Lovers and Gamblers**	Jackie Collins	£2.25p
☐	**Sphinx**	Robin Cook	£1.25p
☐	**Ragtime**	E. L. Doctorow	£1.50p
☐	**Rebecca**	Daphne du Maurier	£1.75p
☐	**Flashman**	George Macdonald Fraser	£1.50p
☐	**The Moneychangers**	Arthur Hailey	£1.95p
☐	**Secrets**	Unity Hall	£1.50p
☐	**Simon the Coldheart**	Georgette Heyer	95p
☐	**The Eagle Has Landed**	Jack Higgins	£1.75p
☐	**The Master Sniper**	Stephen Hunter	£1.50p
☐	**Smiley's People**	John le Carré	£1.95p
☐	**To Kill a Mockingbird**	Harper Lee	£1.75p
☐	**The Empty Hours**	Ed McBain	£1.25p
☐	**Gone with the Wind**	Margaret Mitchell	£2.95p
☐	**The Totem**	Tony Morrell	£1.25p
☐	**Platinum Logic**	Tony Parsons	£1.75p
☐	**Wilt**	Tom Sharpe	£1.50p
☐	**Rage of Angels**	Sidney Sheldon	£1.75p
☐	**The Unborn**	David Shobin	£1.50p
☐	**A Town Like Alice**	Nevile Shute	£1.75p
☐	**A Falcon Flies**	Wilbur Smith	£1.95p
☐	**The Deep Well at Noon**	Jessica Stirling	£1.95p
☐	**The Ironmaster**	Jean Stubbs	£1.75p
☐	**The Music Makers**	E. V. Thompson	£1.50p

Non-fiction

☐	**Extraterrestrial Civilizations**	Isaac Asimov	£1.50p
☐	**Pregnancy**	Gordon Bourne	£2.95p
☐	**Out of Practice**	Rob Buckman	95p
☐	**The 35mm Photographer's Handbook**	Julian Calder and John Garrett	£5.95p
☐	**Travellers' Britain**	} Arthur Eperon	£2.95p
☐	**Travellers' Italy**		£2.50p
☐	**The Complete Calorie Counter**	Eileen Fowler	70p

☐	**The Diary of Anne Frank**	Anne Frank	£1.25p
☐	**Linda Goodman's Sun Signs**	Linda Goodman	£1.95p
☐	**Mountbatten**	Richard Hough	£2.50p
☐	**How to be a Gifted Parent**	David Lewis	£1.95p
☐	**Symptoms**	Sigmund Stephen Miller	£2.50p
☐	**Book of Worries**	Robert Morley	£1.50p
☐	**The Hangover Handbook**	David Outerbridge	£1.25p
☐	**The Alternative Holiday Catalogue**	edited by Harriet Peacock	£1.95p
☐	**The Pan Book of Card Games**	Hubert Phillips	£1.75p
☐	**Food for All the Family**	Magnus Pyke	£1.50p
☐	**Everything Your Doctor Would Tell You If He Had the Time**	Claire Rayner	£4.95p
☐	**Just Off for the Weekend**	John Slater	£2.50p
☐	**An Unfinished History of the World**	Hugh Thomas	£3.95p
☐	**The Third Wave**	Alvin Toffler	£1.95p
☐	**The Flier's Handbook**		£5.95p

All these books are available at your local bookshop or newsagent, or
can be ordered direct from the publisher. Indicate the number of copies
required and fill in the form below   6

Name_____
(Block letters please)

Address_____

_____

Send to Pan Books (CS Department), Cavaye Place, London SW10 9PG
Please enclose remittance to the value of the cover price plus:
35p for the first book plus 15p per copy for each additional book ordered
to a maximum charge of £1.25 to cover postage and packing
Applicable only in the UK

While every effort is made to keep prices low, it is sometimes
necessary to increase prices at short notice. Pan Books reserve
the right to show on covers and charge new retail prices which
may differ from those advertised in the text or elsewhere